The Devil's Captain

The Devil's Captain

Ernst Jünger in Nazi Paris,
1941–1944

Allan Mitchell

Tribute by Volker Berghahn

Berghahn Books
NEW YORK • OXFORD

First published in 2011 by
Berghahn Books
www.berghahnbooks.com

©2011, 2021 Allan Mitchell
First paperback edition published in 2021

All rights reserved. Except for the quotation of short passages
for the purposes of criticism and review, no part of this book
may be reproduced in any form or by any means, electronic or
mechanical, including photocopying, recording, or any information
storage and retrieval system now known or to be invented,
without written permission of the publisher.

Library of Congress Cataloging-in-Publication Data

Mitchell, Allan, 1933-

The devil's captain : Ernst Jünger in Nazi Paris, 1941–1944 / Allan Mitchell.
    p. cm.
Includes bibliographical references and indexes.
ISBN 978-0-85745-114-9 (hbk. : acid-free paper) — ISBN 978-0-85745-115-6 (ebook)
    1. Jünger, Ernst, 1895–1998. 2. Jünger, Ernst, 1895–1998—Homes and haunts—France—Paris. 3. Jünger, Ernst, 1895–1998—Friends and associates. 4. Germany. Heer—Officers—Biography 5. Soldiers—Germany—Biography. 6. Authors, German—20th century—Biography 7. Paris (France)—History—1940-1944. 8. Paris (France)—Intellectual life—20th century. 9. Paris (France)—Biography. 10. France—History—German occupation, 1940-1945. I. Title.
PT2619.U43Z687 2011
838'.91209—dc22

2011000969

British Library Cataloguing in Publication Data

A catalogue record for this book is available from the British Library

Printed in the United States on acid-free paper.

ISBN 978-0-85745-114-9 (hardback)
ISBN 978-1-80073-006-9 (paperback)
ISBN 978-0-85745-115-6 (ebook)

Contents

Preface	vii
Introduction	1
Chapter 1. The Loner	7
Chapter 2. The Road to Paris	14
Photograph Section I	
Chapter 3. Man About Town	20
Chapter 4. Dreaming and Musing	30
Chapter 5. Strange Interlude	35
Chapter 6. Kniébolo and the Nazis	40
Photograph Section II	
Chapter 7. The Plot Against Hitler	47
Chapter 8. Telling Omissions	56
Chapter 9. Immediate Afterthoughts	61
Chapter 10. The Correspondent	68
Photograph Section III	

Postscript. Liebe Sophie	79

Conclusion	90

The Life and Work of Allan Mitchell, 1933–2016	92
    Volker Berghahn

List of Abbreviations	102

Notes	103

Selected Bibliography	119

Name Index	122

Subject Index	125

Preface

Lovers of German literature will immediately recognize that the title of this volume has been shamelessly lifted from Carl Zuckmayer's riveting drama, *Des Teufels General*. For good and explicable reasons, Ernst Jünger was never promoted beyond the rank of captain, and one of the underlying purposes of this book is to clarify why that was so. More important, it is my intention to elucidate why Jünger's comportment as a German officer in the military occupation of Paris during the Second World War was so different from the role performed by Zuckmayer's hero of the German resistance movement.

I first read Zuckmayer's play while a graduate student, working on a master's degree in German literature at Middlebury College in Vermont (where, coincidentally, he was living at the time, before moving to Switzerland). For me, therefore, this study has been a welcome return to a road not taken, since I was soon distracted from literature to the Department of History at Harvard, where I subsequently completed my graduate work. The following years took me through a long circuitous route in Franco-German history of the nineteenth and twentieth centuries, a trail whose final destination was a book entitled *Nazi Paris*. It was the research for that volume that inevitably brought me to an encounter with Ernst Jünger, whose two *Pariser Tagebücher* represent one of the richest, albeit most confounding, records of daily life in the French capital throughout the years of the Occupation. This book, then, can best be read as a sequel and a supplement to my previous work on occupied Paris, which provides a chronological structure to the narrative as well as many of the historical details that were unnecessary to include in this essentially biographical treatment of Ernst Jünger. Here, both as chronicler and participant, he naturally stands on center stage.

Among those persons who have aided me to conceive and correct the final manuscript of this book, I want to single out four close friends: Larry Joseph, once a colleague at Smith College and since then the most intelligent and compatible of Paris hosts; Tom Skidmore, an old Harvard graduate school buddy and squash partner, who later became a distinguished Brazilianist but maintained a keen interest in German history; Klemens von Klemperer, neighbor and mentor of long standing, whose own work on *Germany's New Conservatism* was pioneering; and Annemarie Kleinert, an outstanding historian in Berlin, who made her trenchant criticisms of my writing seem like huge and pleasant compliments. Thanks are also due to Felix Krömer, who allowed me to take advantage of his penetrating *Magisterarbeit* at Berlin's Humboldt University, thereby easing my chores at the German Literature Archive in Marbach, where the Jünger papers are located.

It is a pleasure to pay tribute to two other remarkable personalities and their staffs. Frau Dr. Liselotte Jünger, the widow of Ernst Jünger and a former director of the Marbach archive, was kind enough to grant me permission to make use of some heretofore classified documents housed there. Without that kindness, a key element of my study of Jünger's Paris years would have been missing. Perusal of those papers, I should add, was facilitated in Marbach by the chief of the manuscript department, Dr. Ulrich von Bülow, and by his assistant, Frau Heidrun Fink. The other individual whose support was indispensable for the completion of this project is my dynamic and steadfast publisher, Marion Berghahn, who valiantly agreed for a fourth time to accept one of my manuscripts. At her New York office the help of Ann Przyzycki and Melissa Spinelli was invaluable while bringing it into print.

Finally, I could not close without thanking my family for the love and support that have sustained me throughout many years. It has been a great ride.

Introduction

Very few, if any, critics of German literature would rank Ernst Jünger among the greatest writers of the twentieth century. He simply does not compare, as a novelist, with giants like Thomas Mann, Franz Kafka, or Robert Musil. His signature work, *Auf den Marmorklippen,* has been often justly praised for its chiseled language and allegorical imagination. But for later generations raised on soaring flights of science fiction, Jünger's 1939 work must seem brief, rather stilted, and now somewhat dated. In any event, it pales beside *Buddenbrooks* and *Der Zauberberg, Das Urteil* and *Das Schloss,* or *Der Mann ohne Eigenschaften.* True, the political implications of Jünger's fiction merit scrutiny, but that does not vitiate the commonplace that truly great literary conceptions always transcend the time and place of their authorship.

If Jünger should not be placed in the first rank of German-language novelists, then, he nevertheless surely belongs among the most prolific and perceptive keepers of a journal. Neither "memoir" nor "diary" quite captures the flavor of his published *Tagebücher,* which were frequent and scattered essays worked up from entries he jotted into a small notebook that he ordinarily carried on his daily rounds. The resulting journals were thus self-conscious literary products, carefully edited, written, and rewritten for maximum effect, much as any scholar composes an account based on archival notes with the ultimate intention of publication. Jünger did not write the journals for himself but for a public. To be sure, it is instructive to compare his original versions with the elaborated final text, but he must ultimately be judged on the reconsidered statements that form the corpus of his published work. As he put it himself, "the best record of a first impression is the fruit of repeated efforts, passionate rewriting."[1]

That said, the reader should be aware of the technical difficulties involved in evaluating Jünger's published writings. He was forever tinkering with his prose. His early account of life and death in the trenches of the First World War, *In Stahlgewittern*, appeared between 1922 and 1952 in at least eight different versions.[2]

Similarly, his writings concerning the Second World War evolved through several stages of revision before their printing in the late 1990s as part of Jünger's *Sämtliche Werke*. The German Literature Archive at Marbach am Neckar, near Stuttgart, contains the various manuscripts that preceded a final edition. Despite some overlaps, these versions may be divided into four distinct phases of composition.

Notes: These comprise seven *Notizbücher* (1939–1945) and six *Taschenkalender* (1942–1944), plus a seventh of the latter from 1946. Obviously Jünger carried these pocket-sized notepads with him or had them in his bedroom at night, and scribbled in them randomly to remind himself of quotidian occurrences or thoughts.

Diaries: Seventeen *Tagebücher* (1939–1945) were worked up concurrently or belatedly from the first notations. They assumed the form of logbooks with a day-by-day format that in effect constituted an initial rough draft of what was to follow.

Journals: On the basis of his diaries, Jünger then constructed a fuller edited version that tended to strain out many personal details and include more abstract or philosophical reflections. These handwritten *Journale* are now collected into three leather-bound volumes (1941–1944) at the Marbach archive.

Strahlungen: Under this title the first printed editions of Jünger's wartime observations appeared. They include six sections: one published already in 1942 and called "Gärten und Strassen," describing Jünger's travels in France before reaching Paris; the two "Pariser Tagebücher," recounting his activities in the French capital during the German Occupation; the "Kaukasische Aufzeichnungen," which portrayed a brief interval when he was stationed in Russia; the "Kirchhorster Blätter," entries concerning Jünger's return to spouse and hence Germany near the war's end (these four were initially printed 1949); and finally "Die Hütte im Weinberg," his immediate postwar recollections added to the canon in 1958. Apart from a few interesting amendments and omissions (considered in Chapter 8 of this study) the text of the *Journale* remained essentially the same in the printed *Strahlungen*, which have been given their final resting place in Jünger's collected works published by Klett-Cotta Verlag in Stuttgart.[3]

The unavoidable complications in tracing Jünger's writing through these successive phases should not obfuscate the fundamental fact that his ultimate purpose was to publish his journals, which of course helps to explain many of the changes he made in pursuit of that goal. In reference to all of his wartime recollections between 1939 and 1945, the use of the simple English expression "journals" seems entirely appropriate and harmless enough so long as this more complex background is kept in view.

This treatment of Ernst Jünger's career concentrates on his experience during the Second World War and, specifically, on his role in the German Occupation of Paris, for which his journals constitute the main source along with his extensive correspondence. When correlating and contemplating these primary documents, there are certain basic questions concerning Jünger's comportment before and during the war years that need to be addressed. How far was he willing to go in support of right-wing causes? To what extent did he actually abet those who were sworn enemies of parliamentary democracy? What were his core beliefs in regard to fascism and in particular to Nazism? Moreover, in his personal life Jünger has been accused of an unmistakable coldness toward others. Was that true of his attitude and bearing as a military officer toward his superiors? His inferiors? Toward the French? Or the Jews? If so, did that same chilly disposition color his relationship with women, or did he treat his romantic attachments with a tenderness reserved for them alone? Clearly these are complex personal matters that do not allow simple conclusions or facile formulations. It is surely well for the would-be biographer not to settle prematurely on hard and fast judgments before the relevant evidence has been gathered and pondered. Yet, granted that all readers should reserve the right to form their own opinions, the author of a volume like this has an indispensable responsibility to propose some plausible conclusions while qualifying or rejecting others.

How to proceed? The structure of this book is basically chronological. The first two chapters introduce Ernst Jünger as a young man and retrace the path by which he made his way to Paris in 1941 as a German army captain assigned to the Occupation of France. Chapters 3 and 4 then follow Jünger's footsteps around Paris, considering both his professional and personal contacts, as well as his innermost perceptions that were expressed either in unconscious apparitions while sleeping or in conscious ruminations regularly entered into his journals. Chapter 5 describes the brief but significant episode of Jünger's disturbing experience in Soviet Russia in late 1942, a time that must have removed any uncertainty he might still have entertained about the bestiality of conditions on the eastern front. Chapters 6 through 8 then portray Jünger's return to Paris at the outset of 1943, a period when he became more than ever focused on his relationship to the Nazi regime and to the undeniably charismatic figure of the German Führer. This analysis ineluctably recounts Jünger's marginal involvement in the assassination attempt against Hitler in July 1944, which had immediate and perilous repercussions in Paris. The final two chapters are retrospective, dealing with Jünger's recollections of his Paris years and of the personalities, both German and French, whom he had encountered there.

Finally, a crucial postscript has been added that peers into Jünger's private life during the Occupation. Permission, for the first time, to employ the revealing private correspondence with his intimate Parisian friend Sophie Ravoux enables us to remove many of the ambiguities about Jünger's amorous adventures, ambiguities that previous scholarship had not been able entirely to unravel. This delicate subject of course deserves a reserved and respectful historical treatment, but it is nevertheless an indispensable complement to any biographical account of Jünger's Paris years.

If it is true that Jünger cannot be considered among the greatest German authors of the twentieth century, he was doubtless the most controversial, and the number of articles, essays, and books devoted to appraisals of him is already beyond count. Only a few of them can be mentioned in this introduction; others appear in the endnotes and bibliography.

The earliest German works about Jünger stretched from the frankly harsh recriminations of Peter de Mendelssohn to the learned, albeit somewhat belabored defense of him by Karl-Heinz Bohrer.[4] Positioned between them were two outstanding general studies of the Weimar intellectual scene before 1933 by Kurt Sontheimer and Hans-Peter Schwarz. Sontheimer identified Jünger as one of the many anti-democratic polemicists who emerged after 1918 and who could not escape the charge of thereby becoming gravediggers of the Republic. Casting Jünger as a "conservative anarchist," Schwarz critically analyzed both the style and content of his writings to arrive at much the same conclusion. Together, this pair all but demolished the claim in Jünger's defense that he was merely producing a seismographic record of his time; rather, he actively helped to shape that record.[5] It is no putdown to refer to these early examinations of Jünger's career as pioneering, and their influence was still evident at the end of the twentieth century when more biographical treatments began to appear, such as those by Martin Meyer, Paul Noack, and Steffen Martus, all of whom concentrated less than their predecessors on the problematic ethical aspects of Jünger's activity before 1933 and more on his political and philosophical bent thereafter. They arrived therewith at evaluations of Jünger that can fairly be called balanced.[6]

Yet, by the beginning of the twenty-first century there was still no full-scale biography of Jünger. That scholarly lacuna was soon filled in 2007 by the simultaneous appearance of two 600-page tomes by Heimo Schwilk and Helmuth Kiesel. Without suggesting a whitewash of Jünger, both of them were manifestly well disposed toward their subject, although their estimations of him differed in approach.[7]

Schwilk has produced a rather conventional life-and-times biography from cradle to grave. He sees Ernst Jünger as a perennial outsider who was nonetheless a hard-bitten nationalist and, as such, a committed enemy of the Weimar Republic. Hence, he seems to imply that Jünger was, if anything, rhetorically more radical than the Nazis in his opposition to any participation in the parliamentary process. If there is a weakness in this account, it is the disappointingly hasty treatment of Jünger's activity during the German Occupation of France. The entire period from 1936 to 1943 is handled by Schwilk in a single 25 page chapter in which his geography of Paris is generally fuzzy and sometimes inaccurate (for instance, Jünger's residence in the Hotel Raphael was not located, as he imagines, near the Bois de Boulogne). Still, Schwilk has otherwise made excellent use of Jünger's journals and of the resources at the Marbach archive. He has therewith created a bedrock of Jünger biography that is likely to be budged only slightly in the future.

Kiesel is much more interested in Jünger the writer than Jünger the warrior. As a distinctively literary historian, he tends to move from one of Jünger's published works to another in order to draw a portrait of him as a German *Dichter und Denker*. Thus he devotes nearly sixty pages to an analysis of the composition, revisions, and reception of *In Stahlgewittern* between the two world wars; and the novel *Auf den Marmorklippen* receives twenty pages of summation and criticism. Like Schwilk, he glides over Jünger's four Paris years in less than thirty-five pages, hardly more space than is accorded to his unsuccessful postwar novel *Heliopolis*. It is not surprising, therefore, that Kiesel's main effort is to locate Jünger within the pantheon of twentieth-century European literature by offering extended comparisons with such authors as Goethe, Nietzsche, E. T. A. Hoffmann, Spengler, Thomas Mann, and Gottfried Benn, as well as the French writers Baudelaire, Rimbaud, and Maurice Barrès. While he faults Jünger for an all too permissive attitude toward Nazi war crimes, particularly against the Jews, he insists that such a stance was quite typical of German intellectuals and cautions that one should not exaggerate Jünger's negative influence. It remains to be seen whether this somewhat apologetic appreciation of Jünger will withstand the rebuttals that are sure to come, yet the depth of research by both Schwilk and Kiesel is to be commended and will not easily be gainsaid.[8]

As for Anglophone scholarship, three earlier attempts to introduce Jünger to an international audience are worthy of mention. The 1992 study by Marcus Paul Bullock is an unstructured and rambling treatise that posits Jünger's extreme right-wing position of the Weimar years as the essential starting-point for any interpretation of him. Bullock thereby borders on an unacceptable reductionism, but he manages to sprinkle in some arresting aperçus of Jünger's more important writings.[9] By contrast, the well organized 1999 volume by Elliot Y. Neaman, although marred by far too frequent minor errors, succeeds in presenting a more complex and balanced image of Jünger, which focuses on the political and scholarly reception of his career during the post war era after 1945.[10] These two studies have to some extent crowded out the solid but standard biographical treatment of Jünger's early career by Thomas Nevin, which appeared in 1996 and has now been superseded by Schwilk and Kiesel.[11] In addition, note should be taken of two works by German émigré historians long settled in the United States and writing in fluent English: Klemens von Klemperer and Dagmar Barnouw. Their markedly more critical reading of Jünger is reminiscent of the cluster of German scholars such as Sontheimer and Schwarz, mentioned above. They all place him into the context of antirepublican intellectuals following the First World War, and each chastises him for his cozy relationship with ultranationalism, if not fascism. The ultimate implication of these intellectual histories is cogently stated by Klemperer: "However unwillingly on his part, he was used by the Nazis; however unwittingly, his thought led into the German catastrophe."[12]

In general, one must conclude, despite all the controversy he has aroused in the German-speaking world, and to a lesser extent in France, that Ernst Jünger is a relatively little-known and little-appreciated author elsewhere compared, say, to Kafka or Mann—and he therefore remains a historical personage still to be discovered.[13] Accordingly, the intent of this volume is to introduce Jünger to those who have only a faint impression of him, or none at all, and to explain why he deserves our attention. To do so, the focus here has been shifted from a general biography and sharpened to an optic that affords us a more detailed examination of his experience during the Second World War, undoubtedly the high point of his adult life. As a military officer in the German administration of occupied Paris, Jünger was well placed to observe events in wartime France, and his considerable talent as the keeper of a journal stood him—and consequently us—in good stead. Through his work we are thus able to see Nazi Paris from a specific standpoint, as if viewing it through the lens of a microscope rather than a telescope.[14]

Chapter 1

The Loner

*E*inzelgänger. Not only does the German term for a loner have a more syncopated phonetic rhythm, it also has a distinctly different implication. We think of the English expression as describing a person who spends much time alone and who generally prefers to be alone. Yet that interpretation would hardly include Ernst Jünger, who was very much a man of this world, one who manifestly sought and often enjoyed the company of others. At the same time, as the German word literally suggests, he was an individual who habitually chose to go his own way. This independent streak was in fact quite evident even in his childhood, and it became all the more pronounced as he grew to maturity. As a boy he became a compulsive solitary collector of various things—stones, roots, beetles, insects, butterflies, and so forth—a personality trait still apparent as a grown man in his reading and writing, which retained an idiosyncratic character. In that sense he remained not a joiner but a loner.

Born in Heidelberg on 29 March 1895, Jünger moved with his family before the century's end to Hanover, a middling north-German city around which his life would thereafter revolve. His early education was conspicuously marked by constant movement and indifferent performance. By 1907 he had already attended eight different schools and acquired the reputation of a moody and rebellious pupil. Let it be said that Jünger was by no means the only schoolboy of the Wilhelmine era to suffer under the repressive academic regime of that time, well portrayed in Heinrich Mann's novel *Professor Unrat* and famously adapted for the film *Der blaue Engel*. But Jünger's case seemed to be extreme, and one of his biographers has qualified this early experience as simply "catastrophic."[1] Judging from later references in his journals, the curriculum to which he was exposed consisted of one long course in great books, notably works by Stendhal, Dostoyevsky, Cooper, Mark Twain, and of course Karl May, plus the currently fashionable philosophers Schopenhauer and Nietzsche. How much a disaffected teenager like Jünger actually absorbed from this widely dispersed reading, however, must remain an open question.[2]

Understandably, then, to break away from these unsatisfactory circumstances became for Jünger a strong motivation. More to his liking than the classroom, where he often dozed and daydreamed, was his simultaneous stint in the Wandervogel, a kind of loose woodsy Boy Scout organization that attracted the youth of prewar Germany to hiking and camping. Another significant venture, as it turned out, was Jünger's brief participation in 1909 with a student exchange program in France, where he spent a week in a village between Maubeuge and St.-Quentin, not far from the Belgian border, south of Brussels. There, for the first time, he was exposed to the French language, which was to become one of his major preoccupations as an adult. Meanwhile, he passed on listlessly into an *Oberrealschule* near Hanover, where he read a smattering of standard German literature (Goethe, Schiller, Lessing) and gained a superficial acquaintance with classical authors (Herodotus, Homer, Tacitus). It is important to keep in view that, all in all, Ernst Jünger acquired only a spotty and undistinguished formal education that left him with no systematic grounding in any intellectual discipline.[3]

The most bizarre episode of Jünger's formative years was unquestionably his flight in 1913, at age seventeen, to join the French Foreign Legion. He departed clandestinely from Hanover to Marseille and then shipped out to Algeria armed only with his broken French. No sooner was he forced to submit to the orders of the Legion's officer corps (many of whom were German) than he decided to flee onward to Morocco, where he was immediately captured and imprisoned. Fortunately, his father had useful connections and was soon able to free the terrified boy and return him to Germany, all of which took less than two months and landed Jünger back in school—though not for long. A few months later the Kaiserreich entered the First World War. Jünger promptly enlisted in a local infantry unit, about which he later wrote: "No enthusiasm was so deep and powerful as on that day."[4] Just before leaving for active duty, during his three months of basic training, he was allowed to pass a premature examination for the *Abitur* (normally still a year off for him), the traditional baccalaureate degree ending secondary schooling and providing admission to a university. This wartime improvisation, when he was not yet twenty years old, remained his highest academic achievement—unless one counts a number of honorary titles and prizes awarded him at a senior age.

Jünger was at first stationed in Lorraine near the Aisne-Marne Canal, north of the roadway leading from Reims to Verdun. Like all soldiers on both sides of the conflict, he discovered a war not of movement but of mud. Held somewhat back of the front lines, without encountering a single French combatant, he initially bided his time reading, writing, target shooting, and whoring (about which he was always discreet in his journals). After a seven-week course of officer training, he was assigned to a reserve unit in northwestern France between Arras and Cambrai, an area where he spent most of the war. Although still not yet engaged in heavy combat, he did see death and received his first wound from enemy shrapnel in April 1915, causing a brief debilitating nervous collapse. Recovered, he became a squadron commander (*Fähnrich*), and then in November he was promoted to the rank of lieutenant.[5]

For the next seven months Jünger led a rather idyllic existence behind the front, dining in local restaurants, drinking quantities of Burgundy wine, and courting a French girl named Jeanne Sandemont. After his earlier escapade on a school exchange and his aborted tour with the Foreign Legion, this was his third direct experience with France and the French language. Jeanne proved to be an apt and willing teacher, so that we may date from this period Jünger's passable proficiency as a French speaker. Another activity requires attention. At this time he also began to make regular entries in a notebook to which he confided his personal adventures of wartime, faintly imagining himself as a sort of modern Ulysses, thanks to his recollections of the *Iliad*, read at school. The eventual outcome was an account entitled *In Stahlgewittern*, which would become his first and perhaps most fully realized literary work, to be published right after the war.[6]

The year 1916 brought the Battle of the Somme, the end of his dalliance with Jeanne, and his initiation to sustained frontline military action. Twice more wounded, he was awarded the Iron Cross second-class and shortly thereafter the Iron Cross first-class, before becoming a company commander—not bad for a lad of twenty-one. After a brief tour back in Lorraine, he returned to Flanders fields, where he sustained four more wounds. The last of these was most serious, a shot to the lung. Thereupon he was given the highest possible military award in the Prussian army, *Pour le Mérite*, which became not only his greatest pride, but, as it proved, his surest protection in later life. Let it be noted that during spells of convalescence, under various circumstances, Jünger developed into a prodigious reader, devouring whatever books and other publications happened to fall into his hands. This autodidactic exercise was likewise characteristic of his second passion, collecting insects and beetles that he randomly found while scouring French gardens and woods.[7]

Withal, these events during the war unquestionably constituted for Ernst Jünger the most overwhelming experience of his life. In later years he returned again and again to the earlier forays in combat, and his record of them expressed his best and most basic talent. His later journals, including those portraying his long stay in occupied Paris from 1941 to 1944, thus represented a methodological extension and amplification of his earlier testimony concerning the First World War.[8]

The end of that conflict was of course an inglorious chapter in the history of modern Germany. Still suffering from his lung wound, Ernst Jünger played no notable part in those events, spending much of the war's final months on furlough near Hanover. He could muster no enthusiasm for the revolution of 1918 that sent the Kaiser packing to Holland. Neither could he regret Wilhelm's disappearance, which seemed inevitable. There is no need here to review in detail the postwar working (and later reworking) of *In Stahlgewittern*, except to list three features of it that obviously foreshadowed his future journals. First, Jünger always stands front and center. His recitation is intensely personal in describing the struggles of a courageous young officer at the front. Appropriately, the several editions of this book generally displayed a photo of Jünger wearing a military trench coat unfolded in such a way as to expose his *Pour le Mérite* and the other medals. Second, while the emphasis is on his personal experience as a soldier (there is nothing of grand strategy), Jünger does not neglect to offer occasional philosophical speculations about the larger meaning of the war. Both in style and substance these were certainly influenced by Nietzsche, but even more conspicuously by Oswald Spengler, whose *Untergang des Abendlandes* appeared just as combat came to a close. To a much lesser extent one may find some faint traces of Baudelaire and Rimbaud, who served merely to reinforce a theme of European decadence. Throughout, Jünger's more abstract thoughts had a residue of deep pessimism about a society condemned to pass through fire and despair. Third, as Jünger saw it, the most egregious trait of this unavoidable transition was a mechanization of public life that threatened to eclipse the human element. The age of chivalry is gone, he believed, replaced by trends evident in the evolving nature of warfare—heavy artillery, automatic weapons, tanks, airplanes—and the machine is sure to dominate the world of tomorrow.[9]

These dark thoughts were offset to some extent in 1922, shortly after the publication of *In Stahlgewittern*, when Jünger met Gretha von Jeinsen, a teenager more than ten years his junior, and they suddenly fell in love. Their prolonged courtship and subsequent marriage in 1925 probably determined a number of changes in his personal life. He considerably toned down his excessive smoking, drinking, and experiments with drugs. He also gave up the hyperactive sexual activities that had come so easily to a handsome young decorated officer in the *Reichswehr*. Moreover, he soon abandoned his military career altogether, presumably for good, in order to take up the semi-bohemian existence of a writer. Thus, during the interlude of the Weimar Republic, Ernst Jünger began to emerge as a man.[10] We may add a speculative footnote. In his journals Jünger invariably referred to his wife as "Perpetua," undoubtedly thereby emphasizing her steadfastness as his beloved partner. What he may not have known, since he was not raised as a Roman Catholic, is that this term was commonly applied in monasteries and parish residences to women who performed household chores, sewing, and cooking for priests. Perhaps more than Jünger realized, living in a domestic relationship with more affection than passion, his nickname for Gretha was well chosen.[11]

In the meantime, often at loose ends in his public life, Jünger experienced the years of the Weimar Republic as something of a blur. Like most Germans, he reacted with indignation to the Versailles Treaty, perceiving it as "devastating," and it remained an object of his deep resentment.[12] At the time of the infamous Kapp Putsch in 1920 he was ailing with influenza and took no part. In Berlin he was first attached to the Ministry of War but was bored with the bureaucracy and, as noted, soon resigned from the *Reichswehr*. The first attempt to convert his wartime experiences into literary fiction resulted in a short, mediocre autobiographical novel, *Sturm,* about a young officer at the Battle of the Somme in 1916.[13] Discouraged, he moved to Leipzig and enrolled at the university there as a student of biology. As usual, however, he found no focus and frittered his time away, accurately describing himself as an academic "parasite."[14] Two months in Naples, ostensibly to study marine biology, were spent mostly visiting tourist sites. He did continue to read widely and began to dabble in political journalism, even submitting an essay about "national revolution" that was published in the Nazi Party's main press organ, the *Völkischer Beobachter.* Finally, just before 1933, he completed a curious volume entitled *Der Arbeiter,* which had little or no affinity with Karl Marx aside from an express wish to be rid of bourgeois society. Rather than a proletarian, Jünger's "worker" was a kind of Nietzschean superman caught in a Spenglerian scenario of inevitable collapse. Yet in this pessimistic blend of nationalism and socialism there remained a faint odor of optimism about the outcome. Jünger persisted in seeking some new order that would eventually replace the humdrum republic in which he was living.[15]

After his marriage Jünger returned briefly to Berlin in 1927 with his wife and newborn son, but again he became restless. He took flying lessons, made a quick trip to Paris (where he recorded only a few solemn moments spent at the Tomb of the Unknown Soldier), cultivated some marginal political figures like Ernst Niekisch and Ernst von Salomon, and published a batch of miscellaneous essays—on flowers, fruits, fishes, animals, crystals, books, dreams, etc.—which he entitled *Das abenteuerliche Herz.*[16] At the least, this volume demonstrated that Jünger could write about something besides war. Meanwhile, he enjoyed a minor literary reputation by the success of *In Stahlgewittern,* which was later translated into English (*Storm of Steel*), as well as Spanish and French. When asked, he typically proclaimed his work to be "part of Germany's moral and intellectual armament for the next war."[17]

Doubtless, the likelihood of a future armed conflict was considerably enhanced by the Nazi seizure of power in 1933. Although he found no reason to lament the departed republican regime, Jünger was hardly tempted to join Hitler's victorious movement and instead adopted his customary stance of individualism. As he put it himself: "Thus I provisionally take up the position of an outsider."[18] The only blemish in that statement was the adverb. In truth, there was nothing provisional about his unwillingness to support a dominant political program. Rather, ever the loner, he kept his distance from Nazism—a complex issue that will later require further examination. Did he, then, as some have suggested, undergo an "inner emigration" in the 1930s? Surely this term is inappropriate here, since it implies that Jünger silently and secretly displaced his allegiances, whereas he remained, as before, an inveterate non-participant.[19] This stubborn indifference to German political organizations was reinforced by his move at the end of 1933 from Berlin to Goslar, a town where he readily adapted to the slower pace of provincial life, far removed from the "electric" atmosphere of the capital city. This was even more the case in 1936, when he took up residence in the village of Überlingen on Lake Constance. It was there that he finished a second version of *Das abenteuerliche Herz*. This book appeared in 1938, soon after another rapid (and undocumented) visit by Jünger to Paris and just prior to the height of the Austrian and Czechoslovakian crises. While he was beginning composition of what became his most acclaimed novel, *Auf den Marmorklippen*, the decision was made to move back to the Hanover region. With Gretha and now two sons, Jünger thereafter called home the hamlet of Kirchhorst, one of the evident attractions of which was a location that provided a possible recall to military service with his old regiment. The Jünger family arrived there in the spring of 1939, only a few months before the German invasion of Poland.[20]

Work on the *Marmorklippen* was completed right before the onset of the Second World War. This fantasy, which a modern reader might associate with the tenor of a tale like Tolkien's *Lord of the Rings*, was a chronicle of advancing barbarism led by an evil *Oberförster* from the northern highlands who spread terror through nocturnal arrests and tortures. Rising in opposition, Prince Synmyra and an enigmatic character named Braquemart undertake an expedition to kill the monster but are captured and decapitated, their severed heads displayed on stakes. However a reader might react today to Jünger's story, at the time it was received by many as a kind of astonishing and wondrous fairy tale that, moreover, had possible political implications. It is of course feasible to interpret this 150-page novel as an elaborate allegory of the Nazi regime and the catastrophic consequences that were certain to result from it. Some have wondered why it was not censored by the Ministry of Propaganda, and Jünger later stated that his book was intended as a warning against unrestrained political power. Yet it can also be understood—as he repeatedly insisted—without those specific implications, that is, merely as a prophecy of inevitable struggle from which disaster might ensue. Any such interpretation, in short, is inescapably soaked with ambiguity. If so, we may see the work as yet another version of Jünger's most essential theme: that the destruction of existing bourgeois society must come, a development that is not to be deplored but endured in order to create a new world. Some critics have viewed the *Marmorklippen* as a brilliant parable, whereas others see it as a frightful bundle of clichés. Creative literature or kitsch? There is no way to adjudicate such a scholarly dispute, which is finally a matter of taste and probably also of political disposition. For further reference, in any event, one may note an ancillary conclusion relevant to Jünger's later comportment in Paris: his assumption that conspiracy against an established authority is likely to fail. Hence it is nobler, or at least more prudent, to pass through a tyranny than to attempt to disrupt it. Above all, he seems to conclude, one must remain true not to a cause but to self.[21]

It was while living quietly in Kirchhorst, two days before the German incursion into Poland, that Ernst Jünger was summoned back to military service and promoted to the rank of captain.

Chapter 2

The Road to Paris

Germany's invasion of Poland at the outset of September 1939 marked the beginning of what became known as the "Phony War" (*drôle de guerre*). After the Anglo-French declaration of war, Allied troops took up positions behind the Rhine and the Maginot Line. Waiting there, they peered across at German units that declined to engage in active combat and refused to budge. Apart from the exchange of sniper fire and a few artillery shells, nearly nine months passed without any notable combat on the western front.

These circumstances left Ernst Jünger with much time to carouse, read, and ruminate. He spent hours tramping through fields and around ponds, hunting for mushrooms and observing bees, flies, and frogs. He also explored gardens, places where he felt especially comfortable and that symbolized for him the ongoing struggles of life. Such thoughts came to him as he watched earthworms squirming through the soil, a painfully slow action that brought to his mind the hardly translatable word *Schmerz*, the unavoidable agony of a striving creature. Of course, Jünger continued his eclectic reading: the letters of Erasmus, a novel by Thornton Wilder, Herodotus and Spengler again, the journals of André Gide, and the conservative French Catholic author Léon Bloy. More significantly, he started a new journal, aptly called *Gardens and Roads* (*Gärten und Strassen*), an extended account of his travels from the beginning of the war to the end of his military operations in late July 1940. In reading these passages one must recall, as always, that he wrote not only for his private edification but with the ulterior objective of subsequent publication.[1]

Jünger's first movements were appropriately uneventful. After a brief furlough with Gretha in Kirchhorst, he bade his wife farewell and traveled with the troops westward to Pforzheim and to the Siegfried Line on the right banks of the Rhine. He caught scarcely a glimpse of the French and remarked that the Germans were suffering more fatalities from automobile accidents than from enemy fire. Along the way, stopping in villages and farmhouses, he picked up books, reading the letters of Hebbel, a biography of Anatole France, a short story by Herman Melville, works by Hesiod and Boëthius, and (regularly) the Bible. The winter was cold and his duties were few. With a pair of binoculars he occasionally spied the French from a great distance. The only casualty in his vicinity was a soldier struck by a sniper bullet. Life, he noted, was better endured with strong coffee and plentiful wine. He did find occasion for some tourism. He visited Karlsruhe, making note there of the "easy girls" (leichte Mädchen), which led him to record some unremarkable reflections on the nature of eroticism. He also proceeded up the Rhine by rail to Freiburg im Breisgau, which he proclaimed to be a "pearl" of a city, nestled on the edge of the Black Forest. Without commenting on Freiburg's gorgeous cathedral, impossible for him to have missed, he instead entered a passage in his journal about a flirtatious exchange with a waitress at a nearby restaurant.[2]

Once returned to his bunker and log cabin on the middle Rhine, Jünger endured another sapping bout of influenza. His reading turned to Henry de Montherlant (whom he would later meet in Paris) and to the memoirs of the elder General Helmuth von Moltke, the cultivated and much admired military hero of the Franco-German war of 1870. In late March 1940 Jünger celebrated his forty-fifth birthday—uneventfully, one must judge, except for the first serious shelling by French artillery soon thereafter, which he described in grisly detail ("I felt the legs of the dead man next to my head").[3] As spring arrived, Jünger's unit moved further down the Rhine to Bruchsal and Friedrichsthal. Still nothing more notable occurred than hiking, practicing his equestrian skills, and reading the memoirs of Casanova—someone else like Moltke, albeit for different reasons, to be envied and admired. Although Jünger incurred slight injuries during a fall from a horse, he was apparently fit again on 8 May 1940, when he was told by a senior officer that Germany's only chance to win the war would be to attack in the West, an announcement sounding much like the rationale for the infamous Schlieffen Plan, which in 1914 had propelled German troops into the First World War. Two days later military operations began against the Lowlands and France.[4]

From this time on, after 10 May 1940, Jünger kept a detailed chronicle of his activities until the end of July. His notations opened with a dream of planes roaring overhead. Awakening, he realized that the sounds were real, as German aircraft passed on their way to Belgium and Holland.[5] He followed the same route, shifting in a northwesterly direction and marching through the

Palatinate to Speyer and Kaiserslautern. He confided to his journal his fears that, as in 1914, he might be kept away from battle. His unit soon reached the Moselle Valley, with its impressive vineyards sprawling on the hillsides of both river banks, and crossed over into Luxemburg and the strip of Belgium north of Longwy. Now Jünger's journal entries began to take on a darker tone as he recreated nightmarish scenes of terrible destruction in a landscape reminding him of grotesque paintings by Brueghel and Bosch. Desolation was everywhere. Entire villages were deserted, leaving a ghostly atmosphere of empty streets and roads. In the fields unmilked cows complained of their painful udders. Nothing moved except for a few squads of marching German soldiers, some refugees, and then a column of about four thousand French prisoners, most of them "colored" (*Farbige*). After traversing the border into France, this sight grew even worse: smoldering autos, wreckage of downed airplanes, hastily dug graves, scattered household utensils, cadavers of dead horses, and everywhere emptied bottles of wine and champagne. "Every incursion of Germanic armies," he noted laconically, "is accompanied by heavy drinking."[6]

Near the end of May Jünger's troop entered Sedan, where German panzers had recently passed, leaving the town badly damaged. To his delight he found a stray bottle of 1937 Châteauneuf du Pape, appreciatively commenting that it was Jacob Burckhardt's favorite wine. He asked a passing officer when his unit was likely to see action. Soon, was the promising reply, near St.-Quentin. Yet already Jünger was oppressed by the stench of death—"dead, dead, dead"—and emotionally shaken. His company marched on through the same terrain where he had crouched in the trenches in 1915. There were more POWs, more human corpses, and as always dead horses and dogs lying about, in addition to the flocks of vagrant animals aimlessly wandering: cows, sheep, chickens, rabbits, cats, turkeys, ducks. Ever high-minded, however, Jünger turned his attention to a lucky find, a four-volume set of illustrations from the Louvre, and his thoughts flew to Paris and also, in free association, to Nietzsche and Burckhardt.[7]

By the beginning of June German panzer units were poised for an assault on Paris. Jünger's infantry division was slated to join them, but "unfortunately" the armored advance was too swift and ground troops were unable to maintain the pace. The dream of breaking through to Paris, thwarted in 1918, was obviously alive and well in 1940, and Jünger decidedly shared it. But he was restricted to riding in outlying fields and occasionally to speaking with provincials there. He learned that the French word for bees is *abeilles*—something he might already have known had he been better acquainted with the Jardin de Luxembourg in Paris. The sound of explosions could be heard in the distance, but he and his comrades never seemed to catch up. Hence his military exercises were limited to more target practice with empty wine bottles. Despondently, he could only remark that whether he saw battle in the Second World War depended entirely on decisions made by commanders beyond his purview. It was out of his hands and without reckoning. What he could not avoid seeing, actual combat or not, was a spectacle of mechanized warfare, bringing death and destruction by dive bombers, flame throwers, and perhaps yet poison gas.[8]

In the night of 7–8 June Jünger arrived in Laon, southeast of St.-Quentin, thereby approaching the road leading from Soissons through Compiègne to Paris, now at a distance of barely 100 kilometers. He had bivouacked near Laon in 1917 and was consequently pleased to be in familiar surroundings. Yet what Jünger now encountered there was extreme summer heat and stifling boredom, punctuated by distant claps of artillery fire to the south along the famous Chemin des Dames that snaked through the killing fields of the First World War. In the center of the city he revisited the citadel, the cathedral, the museum, and the library. He wandered through one of the wealthier neighborhoods and admired the degree of comfort enjoyed by its residents, especially, he presumed, their well-stocked wine cellars. Briefly he was charged with overseeing the incarceration of seven hundred prisoners in the Laon citadel. Otherwise, his only sight of enemy activity was a seldom spotted airplane or the shuddering impact of a few stray bombs seemingly dropped at random.[9]

After a week, Jünger received orders to proceed to Château-Thierry, midway between Reims and Paris. He traveled there by truck via Soissons on the very day that Marshal Pétain formed a new French government and opened negotiations for a Franco-German armistice. France had fallen, and Paris was now declared an open city. But Jünger, though only fifty kilometers away, did not immediately reach the capital. Rather, he stood by and watched as long columns of the German army passed with truckloads of troops, tanks, and medical corps, evoking for him strong emotions about its invincible superiority—feelings that could not fail to fill him, as a military man, with pride. Meanwhile, in the nearby village of Ossommes on the Marne River, he was again ordered to command a unit of guards for prisoners of war ("over ten thousand"), with drawn bayonets and German police dogs. The captured French soldiers, he observed, looked quite defeated, and they asked plaintively for food and news of the armistice. Jünger could only tell them that Pétain had offered terms.[10]

Rather than advance to Paris, Jünger and his unit drifted further southward to Romilly-sur-Seine, upriver from the capital. Curiously, he seemed unaware that Paris had already been entered by German forces. Nor did he at first realize that his recent orders to rejoin his division, from which he had been briefly detached for guard duty, did not mean a move downstream. Instead, unquestioning, he jotted into his notebook two awkward sentences that would have obvious implications for his later service in Paris: "I have long ago learned that one cannot arrange everything. One must limit one's view to the space for which one is responsible." That "one" was clearly the veteran military person that Jünger was and remained. After all, it may be said that the German army was the only organization he had unhesitatingly joined.[11]

The latter part of June 1940 was a quiet time for Jünger, which he spent mostly at Bourges in the Department of the Cher, still far removed, due south from Paris. His diary entries became scattered and inconsequential: familiar scenes of destruction, flirtations with French women, regrets about missing combat, descriptions of gardens, trees, and plants. He learned a new French expression, *flûte à champagne,* and found occasion to use it on 24 June when news of the Franco-German armistice reached him while dining, as frequently he did, at the Restaurant Boule d'Or in Bourges. Wine promptly disappeared from the table, replaced by generous quantities of bubbly.[12] If anything piqued Jünger's interest, it was the pleasant friendship with a divorcée identified in his journal simply as Madame Cécile, who taught him to distinguish between *châtaignier* and *marronnier, goûter* and *déguster,* and *pêcher* and *pécher.* She also introduced him to the colorful names of French flowers like *oeillet de poète, amour en cage,* and *pissenlit.* Their final evening together was on 2 July, when Madame Cécile gave him a letter to read after his departure the next day from Bourges. Discreetly, Jünger did not divulge the contents of this parting epistle in his journal, so that the reader is left to wonder about the degree of intimacy the couple had shared during the fortnight of their acquaintance. Why the deliberate omission? Surely the explanation lay in Jünger's expectation that he would someday publish the journal and that "Perpetua," back in Kirchhorst, would eventually read it.[13]

Three days later Captain Jünger was heading northward once more, marching across the Loire and passing again through shattered towns like Troyes. There was little time for reading or reflection, though he carried with him, of all things, a French translation of stories by Conan Doyle. The only notable event en route was a side trip to Domrémy, where he visited the birthplace of Jeanne d'Arc. Then it was on to Toul ("badly destroyed") and to Nancy in Lorraine, before reaching German-speaking territory at Metz. By month's end his troops had traversed the Maginot Line and paraded back into Germany at Saarbrücken to the accompaniment of a marching band. The conqueror thus returned to his homeland without ever reaching the object of his dreams. Withal, Paris was, as Jünger later wrote, "the only city with which I have a relationship as to a woman."[14]

Yet Jünger had, along the way, fortuitously renewed the acquaintance of a fellow officer who was to play a significant role in his life. Werner Best (born in 1903) was somewhat younger than he and consequently lacked Jünger's formative experience in the First World War. Still, the two shared many of the same vague but stirring notions about an impending "national revolution." Best tended to be the more politically minded of the two, and he proved it by joining the Nazi Party in the early 1930s. As it turned out, Best, who was familiar with Jünger's earlier publications, became in 1940 a senior member of the German military occupation in Paris, with his headquarters at the Hotel Majestic in the Avenue Kléber, a five-minute walk from the Arch of Triumph at the head of the Champs-Élysées. It was this connection that was later to result in Jünger's summons to join the commando staff of the MBF (*Militärbefehlshaber in Frankreich*) as a censor and a kind of cultural attaché.[15]

Ernst Jünger's personal story was of course mixed with that of his company. After a long furlough in Kirchhorst and a perfunctory assignment in the Hanover region, he was returned to France in February 1941 and stationed in the village of Sars-Poteries, south of Maubeuge. He exploited this interlude to arrange a weekend in Paris, where he attended a showgirl review at the Tabarin nightclub on Saturday evening and a religious service at the church of the Madeleine on the following Sunday afternoon. It appears from the ordinary touristic character of this routine account in his journal that Jünger's knowledge of Paris remained quite superficial. That was soon to change. On 24 April 1941 Captain Jünger, on horseback and in full uniform under his steel helmet, passed by the Arch of Triumph, leading his marching soldiers and, for the foreseeable future, entered the city of Paris.[16]

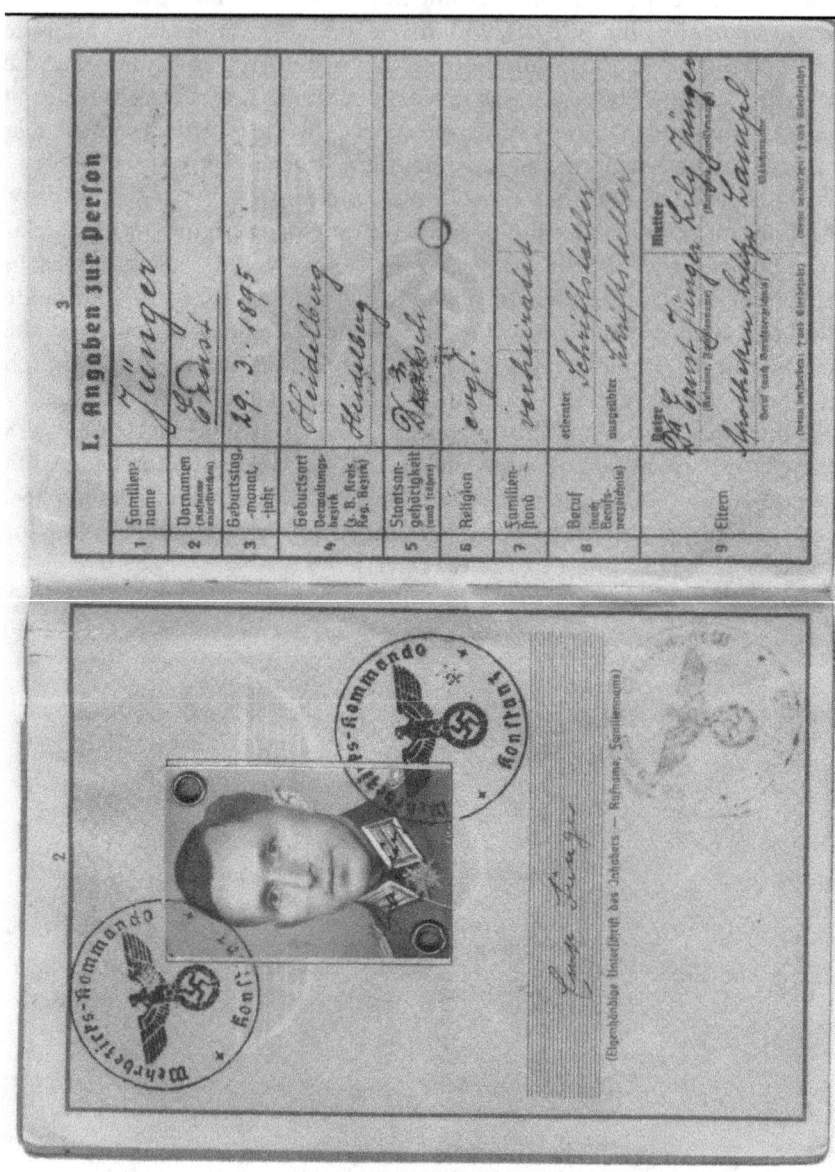

Captain Jünger's military identification card (*Wehrpass*), issued in 1939

(DLA – Marbach)

(DLA – Marbach)

Captain Jünger in 1939

(DLA – Marbach)

Captain Jünger at his desk in the Hotel Majestic, around 1942

Captain Jünger in 1943

(DLA – Marbach)

Captain Jünger in 1944

(DLA – Marbach)

Chapter 3

MAN ABOUT TOWN

Once arrived, Ernst Jünger wasted little time in renewing and expanding his acquaintance with Paris. As his unit was initially stationed at the fortress of Vincennes, on the eastern edge of the capital, he first sought a hotel room at the Porte de Vincennes, whence he could clearly see the obelisk in the Place de la Nation, directly down the avenue to the west, as well as the tip of the Eiffel Tower far in the distance. The following Sunday he moved into a small apartment, with a view of the nearby fort, and passed away a few hours at the zoo of Vincennes.[1] Thereupon began his exploration of Paris: the Hôtel de Ville, the cathedral of Notre Dame, along the quais, up the Boulevard des Capucines to the Opéra, the Pont Neuf and the Pont des Arts, and finally Sacré Coeur. These were already familiar sights for Jünger, as for any tourist to Paris, but the list was lengthened by one novelty less well known. Jünger discovered the Place des Ternes, a five-minute walk from the Arch of Triumph via the Avenue de Wagram. There he selected the Brasserie (La) Lorraine, which he came to frequent regularly, where he could linger on a sidewalk terrace over sandwiches and tea or wine. His predilection for this location was doubtless enhanced on his first visit by meeting a shopgirl named Renée. They dined together and then went to the cinema. "There," he wrote, allowing himself a rare indiscretion in his journal, "I touched her breast." This reverie was interrupted by a commotion in the audience caused by newsreels showing German military actions in North Africa, the Balkans, and Greece. The houselights were turned on, in compliance with regulations from the German military administration, and the couple soon departed. Later, near the Opéra, they separated.

Was that all? As so often, there is no telling. It is certain only that Jünger was visibly warming to the task of occupation.[2]

Two days later Jünger was back at the Brasserie Lorraine, at his favorite table. Again he encountered a young woman wearing a striking outfit of red and blue, but he judged her to be a chilly character, leading him to reflect in his journal on the comforts of being alone, sometimes. He moved on to carouse further in the fancy shops and cafés along the Champs-Élysées, the Faubourg St.-Honoré, and the area around the Madeleine, as well as the Jardin des Plantes on the Left Bank. On 11 May, the day of national observance for Jeanne d'Arc, he chose to mingle with crowds gathered at the Place de la Bastille. He did so in uniform. As it turned out, however, he later became one of the few German military persons in Paris allowed to circulate in civilian clothing, on the grounds that it would facilitate his role as a cultural envoy if he did not always have to appear in regalia.[3]

These bare and banal details of Jünger's first days in Paris with the Occupation are sufficient to establish that his military chores scarcely preoccupied him. He served for a time on guard duty at the Hotel Continental, a post just across the street from the Commandant of Greater Paris, Lt. General Ernst Schaumburg. He also participated now and then in the nearby changing of the guard at the intersection of the Rue de Rivoli and the Rue de Castiglione, and sometimes joined the daily parade of German troops down the Champs-Élysées. He was occasionally involved in police duties, like tamping down disputes between drunken soldiers and irate prostitutes. He attended hearings of a court-martial held at the Continental.[4] To be sure, these events were duly noted in his journal with precise location and presumably accurate date, but they obviously counted far less for Jünger than other occasions such as a dinner on 24 May with Clemens Podewils, a fellow officer whom he had never met but with whom he had previously corresponded. At the table the two were joined briefly by Colonel Hans Speidel (much later a postwar Bundeswehr and NATO commander), at that time a colleague of Werner Best in the Hotel Majestic. This encounter proved to be much more significant for Jünger than he first realized, since it was through Best that he would soon be led to the Majestic.[5]

Parenthetically, one may note another incident of Jünger's early weeks in Paris. In the wake of hearings by the German court-martial, he was ordered to oversee the execution of a soldier convicted for desertion. Overcoming an urge to report himself ill and avoid the assignment, he accepted the duty and, it must be said, fulfilled it with a certain fascination. He learned some details about the accused: that the soldier had been betrayed by his mistress, who sought revenge for being abandoned. Such circumstances were scarcely novel, but this case well illustrated the strict military discipline during the initial phase of the Occupation, when the German administration was attempting to impose order and to impress the French with the correct behavior of its personnel. To witness the event, Jünger traveled to a forest clearing, just south of Paris at Robinson (near Châtenay-Malabry), a site sporadically used for executions by firing squad. With all the skill of a consummate journalist, he created a lurid account of the proceedings and the ghastly sight of the dead victim's corpse. Although these passages have been criticized as an all too graphic rendition of the death scene, they certainly displayed the craft of an experienced writer at work. A more serious criticism has been that this story obfuscated Jünger's own role as commander of the execution squadron by presenting himself merely as an interested bystander.[6]

At the end of May 1941 Jünger found himself at the Hotel Ritz, on the Place Vendôme, in the company of Podewils, Speidel, and a somewhat fawning admirer named Horst Grüninger with whom he was slightly acquainted from social evenings at the Hotel George V. Grüninger expressed his delight at the prospect that Jünger might be permanently assigned to a post in Paris, and there is no doubt that the possibility was brought to Speidel's attention. "Perhaps it would be well," Jünger wrote, "if I took the opportunity to settle down here."[7] This scenario was confirmed by his journal in early June. Learning that he was to be assigned to the MBF staff in the Hotel Majestic, Jünger packed his bags, said farewell to "the amazon" (a cute eighteen-year-old, he specified), and left his Vincennes apartment on 5 June. He commented only: "I saw that Speidel had thought of me."[8] Before taking up his elegant new quarters in the Hotel Raphael, across a side street from the Majestic on the posh Avenue Kléber, Jünger made a long trek to the east of Paris, through a countryside he had previously reconnoitered in February. He returned to Paris on 24 June, precisely three days after the fateful German invasion of Russia, that is, at a moment when the Occupation was entering another and much more troubled phase.[9]

Jünger's residence for much of the next three years was thus the Hotel Raphael, at that time, as today, one of the most princely lodgings in Paris. His office was next door, at the Majestic, headquarters of the MBF staff under General Otto von Stülpnagel, where he served with Werner Best and Hans Speidel. His official assignment was to assist in military censorship, which meant a careful screening of French newspapers and other publications in the occupied territory of France. But, as noted, his far more important function was to act as a kind of cultural liaison to French authors, artists, and intellectuals.[10]

Jünger celebrated his first day back in the capital by returning to his familiar haunt at the Brasserie Lorraine. Conveniently, the Place des Ternes was now barely a ten-minute stroll from his room in the Raphael. That evening he partook of his favorite dinner, a bouillabaisse at the Restaurant Drouant, then loitered for a while at the Café de la Paix next to the swastika-draped Opéra. It was a splendid homecoming, he thought.[11] His journal entries during the early summer of 1941 were filled with notes about incidental acquaintances. One was a curious person named Morris, who had earned his keep before the war by serving as a guide for wealthy British, American, and Scandinavian tourists. With Morris Jünger went slumming on the Boulevard Rochechouart, hard by the Place Pigalle, and listened to his friend dilate on "the technique of erotic advances." Jünger made use of this advice with a Madame Scrittore, whom he met one afternoon at the Place du Tertre. Their conversation became intimate enough for her to confess that she was married to a man who was a good husband but a bad lover. Jünger and she dined that evening beneath Montmartre, at the Place d'Anvers. Whether that was the end of their relationship is unclear, since he made no further reference to it.[12] Inexplicably, he transcribed no entry at all into his journal between 19 July and 8 October. The only explanation offered as he resumed writing was that he, not alone, had been suffering after the opening of hostilities with the Soviet Union from "a sort of spiritual weakness"—an impenetrable statement that perhaps suggested a reason for the beginning of a new project, a systematic daily reading of the Old Testament, which Jünger began on 3 September 1941 and did not finish until 17 April 1943.[13]

It is appropriate to insert a brief reference here to the changing public atmosphere in Paris that was meanwhile occurring. The German invasion of Russia had voided the Nazi-Soviet Pact of 1939, which heretofore had restrained the resistance activities of the French Communist Party. Accordingly, a string of assassinations of German military officials began on 21 August, when a naval cadet was gunned down at the Rochechouart-Barbès metro station. In response, French hostages were rounded up and several were shot. A downward spiral of murders and retributions ensued. It was into this excited and increasingly dangerous scene that Jünger stepped as he took up his post at the Majestic.[14]

This garish backdrop must be kept in view when considering Jünger's recitation of his peripatetic sampling of exclusive salons in Paris. With Speidel, for example, he spent an afternoon at the residence of Vichy's diplomatic representative in the capital, Fernand de Brinon, who occupied palatial quarters near the Étoile. There Jünger learned that the ambassador's wife was inconveniently Jewish, which did not prevent Brinon from using the vulgar expression "*Youpins*" (kikes). Jünger was also introduced to the fashionable playwright Sacha Guitry and to the famous French actress Arletty, whose film (fittingly entitled *Madame Sans Gênes*) had recently opened in Paris. She laughed repeatedly and somewhat hysterically, he noted, at the word "*cocu*" (cuckold). Certainly it is safe to conclude that Jünger was diligent in performing his primary duty to promote collaboration by hobnobbing with France's cultural elite.[15] The list of such individuals was long and ever lengthening. At the apartment of Rudolf Schleier, first assistant to the German ambassador Otto Abetz,

Jünger encountered Pierre Drieu la Rochelle, an editor of the *Nouvelle Revue Française*. Their conversation turned to the scandalously leftist novel by André Malraux, *La Condition Humaine*, which during the Occupation it was acceptable to discuss but not to praise. On more than one occasion Jünger likewise chatted at length with the publisher Gaston Gallimard and the multi-talented genius Jean Cocteau (who was "amiable, suffering, ironic, delicate," as Jünger he later wrote), whom he then visited at the latter's dwelling in the Rue de Montpensier near the Palais Royal. Decidedly, in short, Jünger was getting around Paris, and to retrace the footsteps in his journal is consequently an excellent method to discover the finer sections of the inner city.[16]

Jünger also cultivated members of the military administration and visited German scholars and intellectuals. He frequently saw Hans Speidel, with whom he passed an agreeable afternoon at the Paris flea market (*marché aux puces*), and Werner Best, who on occasion presented Jünger with books to read. Jünger often joined the regular evening gatherings at the Hotel George V. There, besides Speidel, Grüninger, Podewils, and episodically the noted legal theorist Carl Schmitt, he struck up an acquaintance with the historian Friedrich Sieburg, whose impressionistic *Wie Gott in Frankreich*, first published in 1929, had brought its author instant celebrity. The two were in agreement that France, though enduring an irreversible decline, was likely to continue to lead Europe in good taste and high culture.[17]

A cogent summary of Jünger's private life in Paris—in other words, more precisely, his love affairs—is fraught with difficulty. Ever reticent in his journal, he took special pains to mask the extent of his involvement with an attractive pediatrician by the name of Sophie Ravoux. Sufficient evidence has been presented to confirm that Jünger was a *grand charmeur* with a roving eye, whose interest in and success with the opposite sex was indisputable. But diligent researchers have uncovered that many of his specific references to female companions were in fact pseudonyms for Sophie, for which there was evidently a double motive. The first was of course to lessen the blow to "Perpetua," who would probably learn later in Kirchhorst that some of Jünger's deepest affections were elsewhere. The second was to protect Sophie herself, who was ordinarily referred to as the "Doctoresse," since she was of German Jewish origin and married to a French journalist from Lorraine who was picked up by the Gestapo because of his anti-fascist views and who spent much of the wartime in Nazi jails or concentration camps.[18] Hence the frequent contacts with Sophie became parceled out in Jünger's manuscripts and published journals to various personalities called Madame d'Armenoville, Madame Dancart, Camilla, or Charmille. Several of these may have been modeled on women with whom Jünger had a passing but not intimate acquaintance. Charmille, for instance, was given the distinct personality of a mature woman whose wit and wisdom the aging Ernst Jünger came to appreciate; and she was even accorded a private address in the Rue de Bellechasse near the Gare d'Orsay.[19] A few other women were portrayed by Jünger as identifiably real characters, such as one Jacqueline, a fashion designer from Basque territory near the Spanish border, whom Jünger found occasion to visit in her tiny apartment at the Quai Louis-Blériot, in the sixteenth arrondissement opposite the Statue of Liberty on the Seine.[20] Fact and fiction are impossible to parse entirely, even though Sophie's correspondence with Jünger has recently been made available; hence the full extent of Jünger's involvement with her must remain a subject of speculation. Yet what is certain is that during the Paris years he was implicated in a triangular relationship with Gretha and Sophie that resembled a delicious postwar British film entitled *Captain's Paradise* (which involved the philandering hero, suavely played by Alec Guinness, not in frequent passages across the Rhine but the Straits of Gibraltar).[21]

Keeping a journal, not only when it came to matters of the heart, was the form of writing that suited Jünger best, allowing him to flit from topic to topic without full explanation or transition. Many, indeed most, of his entries during late 1941 were brief and cryptic, often containing abstract reflections without obvious reference to the daily routine of events in Paris. One example should suffice. After bringing up the name of Marat, famously murdered by Charlotte Corday in a bathtub, Jünger expounded on the fact that assassination attempts often depend on accidental circumstances and cause unanticipated consequences. So it was with the Archduke Franz Ferdinand at Sarajevo in 1914. While the past is solid, he observed none too profoundly, the future is liquid. Whereupon, mixing metaphors, he added that life is like a card game in which some hands have been dealt while others remain hidden in the deck. Then it was on to another matter.[22]

In December Jünger was granted a leave of absence and traveled back to Kirchhorst to spend Christmas with his family. On 2 January 1942 he shared dinner with Gretha and caught a night train for Paris. In his compartment, returning from a tour in Russia, was a German officer who told a tale of bitter cold, frozen limbs, and amputations—one of several testimonies Jünger gathered over the months that left no doubt about the severity of conditions in the Soviet Union.[23] Once in Paris, he immediately rejoined Sophie and resumed his accustomed rounds in the city: a respite at the Brasserie Lorraine, a saunter down the Rue du Faubourg St.-Honoré, an evening with the regulars in his circle at the George V. In the meantime he widened his already extensive coterie of acquaintances. Attending an elegant soirée at the salon of Madame Boudot-Lamotte, he listened to Jean Cocteau's reading of a new play, met Cocteau's lover, "the actor [Jean] Marais," and chatted with Gallimard and the Doctoresse. This led to his joining a gathering at the Hotel Ritz with the German sculptor Arno Breker, who was presenting a much publicized exhibition of his work in Paris. He also met Claus Valentiner, serving the Occupation as a translator, and was invited to his apartment on the Quai Voltaire, thereafter one of Jünger's preferred hangouts. With the Doctoresse he returned in early February, spending one of many evenings peering over the rooftops of the Latin Quarter and St.-Germain-des-Prés (on this occasion with Cocteau). The domestic comforts of Kirchhorst seemed far away.[24]

The scene in Paris noticeably darkened in 1942. On 8 February Jünger visited Hans Speidel, who shared with him some confidential information about the worsening war in the East and apparently also about Berlin's intentions to deport European Jews to camps in Poland. Whether Speidel explicitly mentioned the infamous Wannsee Conference, held barely a fortnight before, was left unstated. Yet, even when Hitler's plans were seen through a veil, Jünger could have had little doubt that the Final Solution was beginning in earnest and that it was soon to be extended to France. "Doubtless there are individuals," he wrote, "who are responsible for the blood of millions." If so, Jünger commented, the truth was that many Frenchmen approved and were willing to join in.[25]

The seriousness of the situation was underscored by an afternoon Jünger spent with the reigning MBF, General Otto von Stülpnagel, in late February. His nerves obviously frayed, Stülpnagel was preparing to leave Paris in protest over the notorious hostage crisis. After the assassination of German officials in Nantes and Bordeaux, Hitler had ordered that one hundred Frenchmen be executed for every German murdered in France. Stülpnagel contended that such drastic measures were incompatible with his assignment to ensure an orderly Occupation in Paris. Berlin's policy, he thought, would only perform a great service for the French Resistance. Nevertheless, it must be said that he had expressed no moral reservations about taking the life of hostages and had indeed suggested that many of them should be deported "to the East," tantamount to a delayed sentence of death. As for Jünger, he considered the general's position to be only rational, an attitude that accorded with his own long-held view that the old aristocracy and educated bourgeoisie of Germany were being displaced by "those who know nothing else besides power"—a central theme of Jünger's novel *Auf den Marmorklippen*.[26]

These remarks melded in Jünger's mind with increasingly frequent reports about brutality and mass killings in Eastern Europe. It was like a great illness, albeit one that could eventually be cured. Otherwise (that is, if there were no cure), he claimed, he would immediately desert the army—a dubious, not to say empty, threat.[27] On 10 March Jünger passed an evening with the new MBF, Otto's cousin Heinrich von Stülpnagel. The two were to become fast friends. Heinrich was well suited to calm ruffled feelings in Paris. He was much more patrician in bearing than his namesake, and he displayed a quality of *désinvolture*—a sort of superior casual disinterestedness—that Jünger much admired. In fact, Jünger liked to think of himself as possessing that same trait, although there were those who mistook it for coldness.[28] Let it be appended here that Jünger's scattered notations at this time on what the Germans invariably called "the Jewish question" (*die Judenfrage*) did not implicate him in anti-Semitism. If anything, he was appalled by rumors reaching Paris about extermination and euthanasia programs, which would not suppress Jewishness, he wrote, but enhance it. At most, not for the first time, he may be charged with ambiguity.[29]

In the spring of 1942 Jünger was granted a six-week furlough. Before leaving Paris he again made a tour of his usual social contacts, especially Sophie and his confidant Hans Speidel. On the eve of his forty-seventh birthday he attended the salon of a wealthy American lady, Florence Gould, to whom he would become attached. It was a sign of the times that this soirée was interrupted by an air raid alarm and ended with candles, champagne, and somber talk of death.[30] As if Jünger were leaving Paris for good, an elaborate farewell party was arranged at the Quai Voltaire by Claus Valentiner. It was attended not only by some of Jünger's German comrades from the Hotel Majestic but also by French luminaries such as Cocteau and Drieu la Rochelle—evidence enough that his efforts in behalf of Franco-German collaboration had not been in vain. Jünger departed by rail from the Gare de l'Est on 7 April and traveled to Mannheim, where he was met by Speidel, also on leave. Then it was on to Hanover, Kirchhorst, and Gretha. Once more his journal became a virtual blank, with only infrequent entries concerning his incidental reading and occasional letters from Paris. In other words, Captain Jünger was at home, not to be disturbed.[31]

Jünger's reappearance in Paris in late May 1942 started where it had left off, chez Valentiner on the Quai Voltaire, where the likes of Jean Cocteau and Jean Marais were present. One may easily divine his other visitations and contacts as he took up residence once more in the Hotel Raphael. We may add three venues to that list: first, St.-Rémy-les-Chevreuses (repeatedly written by Jünger without an accent mark), a charming village at the terminus of the capital's first and most famous suburban railway, the Ligne de Sceaux; second, the most glamorous of Paris restaurants, the Tour d'Argent, overlooking the Seine behind Notre Dame ("In such times, eating, good and plentiful eating, lends a feeling of power");[32] and third, not unknown to Jünger, Maxim's. It was there, after he left a lunch at Maxim's and stepped onto the sidewalk of the Rue Royale, that he first witnessed the yellow Star of David, worn by three passing Jewish girls. "I suddenly felt embarrassed to be in uniform," he confessed. From Sophie he learned that non-Jewish students had protested the stars by donning them while promenading on the Champs-Élysées, not a prudent action in Paris by the middle of 1942. Jünger remarked that these students were like children waving flags as they entered water infested by sharks. No exaggeration, his statement was amply confirmed on 18 July when the great "Vel d'Hiv" razzia was unleashed and thousands of Jews were caught in the Nazi net. There was "wailing in the streets," Jünger recorded without passion or overt criticism. His own pleasant existence in Paris would of course continue, he wrote, but not without the surrounding misery of others. It was a noble thought perhaps, but also evidence of humanism at arm's length.[33]

Jünger's routine was well established by now: mornings at his office in the Majestic, afternoons exploring the city and especially its bookshops, then convivial evenings dining and strolling. A few events stood out. More than once he visited the fabled cemetery of Père Lachaise with "Charmille," taking particular note there of the tombs of Oscar Wilde, Cherubini, and Chopin, while portentously concluding that "life lies amid death like a small green island in a dark sea."[34] He also frequented the cemetery of Montparnasse, seeking out the gravesite of his favorite pessimist, Charles Baudelaire. Likewise, he paid his respects to the living and still very energetic Pablo Picasso at his studio on the Rue des Grands-Augustins, not far off the Boulevard St.-Michel, in the Latin Quarter. As he displayed his current projects, the artist asked Jünger about the actual locale of the *Marmorklippen* (no word of the answer); otherwise they engaged in small talk.[35] More significant were Jünger's evening walks with the Doctoresse, during which his thoughts inevitably turned to Romanticism. This was the case one night as the couple approached the equestrian statue of Henri IV at the western tip of the Île de la Cité, where they descended the adjacent stone steps to the Square du Vert-Galant. Characteristically, Jünger painted this episode with moonlight and intimations of eros, but he neglected to mention in his journal how the stroll concluded.[36]

In mid-August Jünger passed a weekend at Vaux-les-Cernay, southwest of Paris near Rambouillet, as the guest of the new commanding general in France, Heinrich von Stülpnagel. Little was recorded of their conversations except a discussion of the relative merits of the English and the Prussians, a sea-folk and a land-folk. Another of Stülpnagel's remarks, however, stuck in Jünger's mind: maybe it would be well if he served some time with German military forces in the East. Jünger seemed to agree, but then the matter was dropped.[37] News of the war was hardly encouraging, and he was out of sorts. Reports arrived early that autumn of the devastating fire bombing of Hamburg, which caused him sleepless nights. In September, just as the war was entering its fourth year, he learned of the destruction of Cologne. The Nazi military machine was being revved up to the maximum, and hundreds of thousands of French workers were being recruited for labor in German factories and farms. Restless, Jünger did nothing for the time being but retrace his rounds in the city: the Bagatelle Park in the Bois de Boulogne, bookstores in the Rue du Faubourg St.-Honoré, the Quai Voltaire, the Ritz, St.-Rémy-les-Chevreuses, Vincennes (to visit his old concierge), the Place des Ternes, and the Place du Tertre, where he dined at the Restaurant à la Mère Catherine and slipped into the basilica of Sacré Coeur. No wonder he summed up: "The city has become a second spiritual home to me."[38]

Letters from his wife did little to cheer him up. She predicted that the second half of the twentieth century would be even worse than the first. "I do not want to believe it," Jünger wrote, but who could tell when the war would end? He spent a long evening with the Doctoresse, who heard him out in a kind of psychiatric consultation, "since I have been dissatisfied with my circumstance." He was losing weight and, so he thought, suffering from melancholy. He continued to sleep badly at night and whiled away his daytime hours with long promenades. He even took up horseback riding again in the Bois de Boulogne, where the trees were displaying the brilliant foliage of autumn.[39] Such was his mood when he was told that his transfer to Russia was an imminent possibility. Not surprisingly, his response was one of relief. As a boy he had fled the tedium of schoolwork to join the French Foreign Legion, and now he might escape his petty duties in the military administration in Paris for an adventure in the Soviet Union. If only he were not so ill. Jünger's insomnia worsened and, on doctor's orders, he was admitted to a clinic in the western suburb of Suresnes. From his bed he had a splendid view of the nearby Mont Valérien—where, we know, hundreds of hostages and other undesirables were executed by firing squads during 1942, a fact of which Jünger made no mention in his journal. Besides Claus Valentiner and a few other friends, he was visited in the clinic by the Doctoresse, bearing flowers. To this affectionate gesture he registered a self-revealing comment: "My tendency, when I love a person, [is] to distance myself from him."[40] Meanwhile he suffered from attacks of what he called "*la frousse*," a term that may be translated as fear, alarm, or angst. When released from the clinic, he received a diagnostic notation of "*anacider Magenkatarrh*," a medical term for a condition similar to a stomach ulcer. Still ailing, he decided to seek out a French physician, who helped him more than the clinic, he estimated, and who, upon hearing that Jünger was about to leave to fight against Bolshevism in Russia, refused to accept a fee.[41]

It remained only to say farewell to Paris. He took official leave of his superior officer and personal friend Colonel Karl-Richard Kossmann at the Hotel Majestic. He also said goodbye to the MBF, Heinrich von Stülpnagel, about whom he was moved to say that "the General counts among those persons who entered my life as an unexpected gift," words to remember in the light of later events. Nearly ready to depart, Jünger attended a religious service (probably at the Madeleine), wandered one last time through the Rue du Faubourg St.-Honoré, and met with his French companion Sophie Ravoux near the Place des Ternes. But their parting tryst was interrupted by an air raid alarm. Jünger needed to leave early in any event, lest he miss his overnight train to Berlin.[42]

Chapter 4

DREAMING AND MUSING

Looking back across the time of his first tour of duty in Paris during 1941 and 1942, it is striking how much space in Ernst Jünger's journal was devoted to dreams. Dozens of entries recounted dream sequences in which Jünger, ever at the center of things, underwent some remarkable imaginary experience, which he hastened, once awake, to record in detail.[1] Even Sigmund Freud, however, would have been hard pressed to reconstruct a coherent interpretation of all these accounts. There are several obvious difficulties in attempting to do so. First, one must always make allowance for Jünger the skillful writer. It is impossible to unscramble the occasions when he was merely reciting the literal contents of a dream or when he was embellishing such images with his considerable literary talent. Notoriously, memory is a slippery matter. Second, as Jünger noted more than once in self-criticism, there is forever a problem of distinguishing between dream and reality. Many of his sleeping perceptions were of course triggered by actual events and daily occurrences, and in the final version presented in his journal it is often impossible to tell one from the other. Third, Jünger was at times an insomniac who spent restless nights, half awake, during which he "only dreamed or mused" (*während ich doch nur träumte oder sann*).[2] In precisely what state of consciousness he existed when certain images or ideas came to him was a mystery—first of all to himself, and accordingly to us. Evidently, then, a full measure of caution is in order while exploring the territory of Jünger's imagination where the boundary between dreaming and musing remains indistinct.

Although a consistent rational pattern might therefore be ruled out, it is feasible to identify some recurrent features of Jünger's dream world. Naturally, many speculations of the sleeping mind were induced by personal experiences, such as the time he harbored dark thoughts about "the cold mechanism of power" when awakened one night by the roar of an automobile engine or, as noted, when his dream about the sound of airplanes passing overhead proved to be real. Such events could be immediate or distant, like scenes of battle, marching, and riding in an elevator (all recent), but his dream of standing in damp rat-infested trenches was reminiscent of an experience in war long before. Not surprisingly, these dreams included erotic fantasies, for instance, of a beautiful woman kissing his eyes, another feeling his body with her long fingers, and a third who remained desirable even after being beheaded. Thus the events of Jünger's actual life while reaching and residing in Paris were refracted into imaginary recreations of them in his dreams.[3]

The same was true of the family. Without question, the person who most frequently appeared to Jünger in his dreams was his aging and ailing father, usually as a beloved but not especially affectionate patriarchal figure. Far less prominent were his mother and his wife. Did they disturb Jünger's sleep less often because they were female or because they were far less imposing? Perhaps a professional psychiatrist might venture an answer, but the historian must demur, except to note that the male parent was Jünger's most regular night visitor.

Friends also played a role. Carl Schmitt, for example, appeared in one dream in a train station where he had fallen and was injured, with much weeping. Others would come and go, on which Jünger commented that he seemed to dream particularly of those whom he had somehow wronged and from whom, once so portrayed, he felt rewarded by their forgiveness.[4]

There were dreams of high adventure, like a voyage through Tibet, and also dreams of premonition: "Often experiences appear to me as if I had previously dreamed of them."[5] Yet the most persistent theme of what can only be called nightmares had to do either with feelings of helplessness or else decadence and death. These took many forms: Jünger is a prisoner condemned to death; he is trapped standing in water; he is climbing a rock cliff in mortal danger of falling; or there is a flood in which the waters are infested by snakes that must be fought off with a stick. Some of these scenes, as Jünger observed, were elaborately Bosch-like, with animated tableaux of naked people being harassed by their torturers and executioners.[6] Apparitions of vipers were common in Jünger's recounting, invariably slithering symbols of menace and malfeasance. Certainly it is fair to assume that a pronounced dread of death haunted Jünger's subconscious, as when he closed his eyes and saw himself in a dark landscape "on the edge of infinity." This sense of foreboding was related in turn to repeated impressions of hopelessness. Such emotions, it is important to reiterate, lay somewhere in a no-man's land between dreaming and musing, of which the only remaining trace is Jünger's own unreliable record of them.[7]

As we saw, Jünger's final weeks in Paris, before leaving for Russia, were marked by illness and frequent attacks of insomnia. At times he reached a degree of delirium in which, more than ever, he had difficulty in distinguishing between moments of waking and sleeping. As a consequence his journal became even more fragmentary than usual and the reporting of dreams kaleidoscopic. Images crowded in: visiting an unkempt garden to view Gothic structures; lying like a mummy in a wartime trench; a golden swordfish; massive clouds rolling by; climbing a mountain to reach a chapel in the heights; observing soldiers who received small round medals for performing their service of shooting the wounded; and, as in the past, the appearance of his beloved father as a messenger of melancholy and likely a harbinger of death. What is the bewildered reader to make of all this? Jünger is not much help as an interpreter, lying in his clinic bed dreaming and then musing for a long while in a vain attempt "to separate this mirage from reality."[8]

Truth to tell, Jünger's waking thoughts were not appreciably more coherent than his dreams. He cannot be said to have developed an identifiable philosophy or political theory, either of which would have stood in contradiction to his inveterate and self-acclaimed individualism. Furthermore, his favorite mode of expression, the daily journal, militated against any systematic elaboration of a single intellectual scheme.[9] Once again, therefore, in attempting to analyze his musing beyond the myriad of dreams, one must be content with sorting through bits and drabs of thought. At least, while doing so, certain positions or points of emphasis do come to light. Here they may be limited to five.

First, Jünger was acutely aware that European society was undergoing what he called "a general transition to automation."[10] This observation followed from his frequently repeated declarations about the advance of technology and mechanization, most obvious in warfare, of which he had direct experience, but also throughout modern life. Jünger recalled his first ride on the German Autobahn and declared it to be a fitting symbol of modernity. Therewith, inevitably, one must expect increased regimentation. Individual action still counted for something in this process, but the threat existed that the efforts of a few would be overwhelmed by a crushing weight of the automatized many. "The sight of the masses," he wrote, "is oppressive."[11] The same notion occurred to him when he learned in September 1942 of the destruction of Cologne, which represented for Jünger a triumph of *Amerikanismus,* that is, of vulgarity. It cannot be said that such ideas were particularly original, bearing as they did close similarity, among others, to the gist of Oswald Spengler's long essay "*Preussentum und Sozialismus,*" already published in 1919. But Jünger's perceptions, regularly updated in response to recent events after 1933, nonetheless constituted a core element of his thinking.[12]

A second recurrent theme in Ernst Jünger's journals was the increasingly prominent role of religion. This clearly went hand in hand, whether by cause or effect, with his daily readings of the Bible. Jünger's was a generalized religious belief ("God is present") rather than a theological one attached to church dogma (raised as a rather agnostic Protestant in a mixed family, he converted to Roman Catholicism late in life). Besides, his ill-defined mystical faith was always balanced by a positivistic tilt toward Darwinism, inherited from his father. Maybe, after all, he retained from his early and embarrassingly perfunctory study of botany a residue of belief in natural history and, by extension, a conviction about the struggle for survival of the fittest. Given the disorderly form in which his views were expressed, it may be fatuous to attempt to untangle Jünger's religious predilections. Perhaps the most that one can conclude with confidence is that he felt most comfortable while musing in a tended garden where God and nature could peacefully coexist.[13]

Third, speaking of tended gardens, it is conspicuous how often Jünger contemplated the rewards and restraints of a bourgeois existence such as the one he knew with Gretha in Kirchhorst. Living at home obviously afforded him great pleasure, and more than once he would allude to the gratification he felt while being spoiled by his wife's notable "domestic skill" (*Hausfrauenkunst*).[14] Yet Jünger's placid demeanor was constantly torn by his passionate and confounding lust for adventure. He once contrasted the quiet homey routine assured by Gretha with the imaginary thrill of discovering treasures in an unexplored mine in Peru. The dilemma was most poignantly expressed in a journal entry in which Jünger depicted parting on a night train from Hanover to Paris. Saying goodbye to her uniformed husband, Gretha began to weep and then hastened down the station's platform steps as Jünger's railway car pulled away, bound for France. For him Paris was an adventure to which he gladly returned and that doubtless included a strong erotic factor, which he sought—none too successfully—to contain within the bounds of his marriage.[15]

Another recurring reference in Jünger's journal was to the growing domination of centralized power and, concurrently, the struggle and suffering caused for those attempting to cope with it. This somewhat abstract scenario of course harkened back to his novel, *Auf den Marmorklippen,* and it was no less obviously related to his reactions to the establishment of the Third Reich. This was an ongoing process that entailed both destruction and creation, in that order, which undoubtedly explained Jünger's mood swings of depression and exhilaration. These mood swings were closely involved with his military duties in Paris. From the office of Hans Speidel he received the task of writing an analysis of the pervasive friction between the MBF's administrative staff in the Hotel Majestic and the various minions of the Nazi Party based in the capital. This study led Jünger to investigate the so-called hostage crisis that resulted in the resignation of Otto von Stülpnagel and the succession of his cousin Heinrich. In the course of the inquiry, to buttress his report, Jünger undertook the translation of farewell letters written by hostages just before their execution. It was a deeply troubling exercise, which forced him to confront the roles of love and death—those two great "benefactors" (*Wohltäter*)—in a dictatorial state. Whatever these musings lacked in analytic clarity, they were unquestionably a product of the emotional turmoil that strained Jünger's relationship to the Occupation's regime in Paris and induced him to embrace an escapist assignment with the German army in Russia.[16]

Finally, there was Jünger's interminably disturbing preoccupation with death, whether sleeping or awake. Symptomatic, no doubt, was his uncommon interest in cemeteries, which he took every opportunity to visit, always lingering there over noteworthy tombs and inscriptions. In his journal—ah, the imperfections of existence—he repeatedly made reference to his worries about injustices, disappointments, faults, uncorrected errors, aging, and ultimately physical decay and death. One passage recorded his realization, upon awakening, of a profound sadness that came over him like rain or snow when facing the end of his days and, while still living, "the distance between humans, even those closest to us and most beloved."[17] Specifically meant in this case was his spouse, with his only consolation being that at least death would erase that distance. Presumably this opaque thought provided the context for Jünger's remark in July 1942, when reading Henry de Montherlant, about "the longing for death."[18]

Admittedly, such a rapid exploration of Ernst Jünger's mind, as revealed in his journals, must remain incomplete and insufficient. Yet significant clues recur in abundance, and an attempt to reorder them is worthwhile. His initial extended stay in Paris provided a perfect laboratory to cultivate his intellect and to stir his imagination. With his usually light military duties and his broadening circle of acquaintances, he was free to roam throughout the city with more than enough leisure to record his impressions. If his writing often remained fragmented and cryptic, it was only a true reflection of Jünger's wandering intellect, as well as an appropriate and probably unavoidable consequence of the form of writing that his journals embodied.[19]

Chapter 5

STRANGE INTERLUDE

The route from Paris to Russia of course passed through Germany. As Jünger's train slowly made its way into the devastated city of Cologne, his thoughts turned once more to the detestable triumph of *Amerikanismus,* that great leveler of European culture. Later, as usual, he was met by his wife at the railway station in Hanover and joined her for a pleasant week in Kirchhorst, where he enjoyed reading and gardening as his health seemed to improve. On 10 November 1942 Jünger received news of Operation Torch, the Allied invasion of North Africa, without fully realizing that this event would mark a new phase in the German occupation of France. As Hitler peremptorily informed Marshal Pétain, it would be necessary to erase the Demarcation Line between the former occupation zone and the southern territory, until then nominally under the Vichy regime, by advancing German troops to the shores of the Mediterranean. To occupy the entirety of France was to stretch the military administration painfully thin across the nation and to create a host of new arrangements—and hence frictions—with the French. Of all this Jünger would learn later.[1]

He left with Gretha and his mother by rail from Hanover to Berlin, where they stayed for a few days in suburban Dahlem with Carl Schmitt and took long walks in Grunewald, the city's sumptuous but now partially destroyed West End. Gretha saw him off as he departed for the Soviet Union. He arrived at Kiev by airplane and stayed overnight in the reputed Palace Hotel, known as one of the finest in German-occupied Russia, albeit without running water, as Jünger scornfully noted. When he moved on to Rostov he also observed that Russian currency in circulation still bore a portrait of Lenin. In general, Jünger's first impressions were largely negative. Technical things worked well enough: railways, automobiles, weapons. But in this retrogressive land there was an evident lack of food, clothing, warmth, and light. Hence his initial and lasting experience, in the midst of considerable destruction, was of confusion and cold. This gloomy appreciation could only be deepened by reports that the Russians had broken through German defenses north of Stalingrad.[2]

A relevant curiosity item was Jünger's brief encounter with Major General Ewald von Kleist, commander of German forces in the Caucasus, whom he had known years earlier in Hanover. Rather than dwelling on more immediate and depressing circumstances, their conversation turned to North Africa, where, as Kleist had just learned, the French general Henri Giraud had reached Tunis. Jünger remembered that Hitler (here mentioned, as rarely, by his proper name) had predicted after Giraud's escape from a German prison camp that bad news could be expected from him. It is striking, in light of later events, that Jünger made no reference to Charles de Gaulle, whose name he either did not know or whose future importance he did not anticipate.[3]

Otherwise the daily rounds of Jünger's first weeks in Russia were uneventful and his record of them unremarkable. He resumed his daily perusal of Scripture, which he had suspended since his stay at the clinic of Suresnes in the previous August. He continued the practice of jotting down recollections of his inscrutable dreams, such as one of an auto sporting the ornament of a fantastic animal. He mused about the quality of personal relationships in Russia, speculating without further evidence or explanation that they were more profound than in France. And, as often, he offered some self-evaluation: for instance, that he was comfortable with the lowest or highest exemplars of human intelligence but could not abide middlingness.[4] In sum, while in the war-torn Soviet Union, Ernst Jünger led an aimless and restricted life, usually behind the front lines far from battle in a strange world with which he found little connection. He caught only glimpses of the merciless struggle in progress in which neither side was taking many prisoners. His adventure there was thus mostly second hand, and it was no wonder that he quickly determined that he would not long remain in Russia. Too many places were taboo for him, above all locations where there were executions and reprisals (such as he had witnessed in Paris) or where the unarmed were mistreated. He had to ask himself if it would not be more appropriate to visit these scenes and to see both the perpetrators and victims of such action. True, there were appropriate limits to what might be shown to the uninitiated, but he felt left out of everything concerning atrocities except the talk of them. Typically, he once overheard the laughter of some officers about the shooting of Russian hostages, leading him to remark on "the automatic habit of killing," which he caustically likened to automatic fornication.[5]

As the weeks went by, Jünger's observations and reflections tumbled out in disarray. On the streets he singled out "Mongolian types" with "Asian faces," often pockmarked, in contrast to the beautiful Caucasians. He expounded on the dangers of laying explosive mines, which he took to be yet another symbol of the mechanization of warfare at a time far advanced in that regard from the First World War. The scale of combat, he wrote, had become infinitely greater in a titanic struggle of willpower unknown since ancient Persia faced off against Greece. It went without saying that Jünger assumed the Russian hordes to be comparable to Persians and the Greeks to Germans. These sweeping thoughts were distilled into the image of a dead Russian soldier whom he found lying face down, as if asleep. Troubling emotions of helplessness welled up inside him, "a feeling of being caught in a huge machine where only a passive existence is possible."[6]

On he went, collecting and recording random scenes of slain horses, collapsed bridges, and abandoned corpses. Obviously Russia was for Jünger everything that Paris was not. He missed the bookstores, the fancy restaurants, and the elegant women, finding instead an unfathomably vast space of unmitigated crudeness. He could only dream of his former idyll in France, and did so, his memories prodded by sporadic correspondence from Perpetua, Carl Schmitt, and Claus Valentiner.[7] His celebration of Christmas with a few comrades was accordingly muted, the mood further dampened by outspoken worries among them that the German southern flank might soon collapse, as Hans Speidel had predicted months before. An interesting conversation occurred with a German officer who had once spent ten years in Texas as a chemical engineer working in the oil fields. He predicted that there would be no definitive military decision in Europe but rather a prolonged standoff between the Soviet Union and the United States, at the expense of the British and French empires (not a bad description of the Cold War to come). Jünger disagreed, since he believed that such remorseless violence could only end in victory or defeat for the Third Reich.[8] On New Year's Eve he attended another party, though that was hardly the word for a round of conversations about atrocities that had been committed by the German army after the conquest of Kiev. Rumors were meanwhile circulating that poison gas was being used against Russian Jews. Only rumors, Jünger wrote, but surely there could no longer be any doubt that mass killings were taking place in the East. Once more, much like the day when he had first sighted yellow stars in the streets of Paris, he felt a certain disgust with the uniform he had so long prized. Predictably, he thereupon reiterated one of his well-worn themes about a fading age of chivalry being replaced by an emerging era of mechanization.[9]

At the beginning of 1943 Jünger spent his final six weeks in Russia. The written remains of those days contain no surprise. As always, his journal entries were studded with accounts of dreams, one of which is worth a mention.

In this sequence Jünger found himself in the lobby of a large hotel where he was conversing with a doorman holding silver keys to the luggage. Dimly perceiving that the hotel represented the world and the bags the transient nature of life, he promptly formulated (in the dream?) three resolutions: to be moderate, since almost all difficulties result from excess; to look out for unfortunates, thereby overcoming the human tendency to look away from misery; and not to worry about individual fates in the midst of catastrophe but rather to assure that one's own conduct be honorable and worthy—yet another tribute to rugged individualism. Perhaps it is well not to comment here on the sheer banality of these propositions, which nevertheless express one man's yearning for some guiding principles in the midst of surrounding chaos and deep personal discomfort.[10]

Just how chaotic the military situation was becoming as the Battle of Stalingrad reached its climax was reflected in Jünger's final journal entries before his departure. His contacts with informed commanders and junior officers were frequent enough for him to form a notion of the impending German defeat. That included the undeniable truth that millions had been killed, many of them noncombatant victims of brutal atrocities. Furthermore, the collapse of the army's southern flank could apparently be attributed in large measure to the mistakes of the German high command: "Clausewitz would turn over in his grave."[11] As Jünger began moving back westward, he overtook streams of Ukrainian refugees who had greeted the Germans in 1941 and who were now fleeing for their lives from the Russian advance. He detected widespread pessimism among senior military officials, including Major General von Kleist, who, after the surrender of Field Marshal von Paulus at the onset of February, would assume supreme command of the southern front. Evidently it was from Kleist that Jünger learned that his father, whom he had not seen since 1940, was gravely ill. Obtaining leave, he returned in haste to Kirchhorst, only to find that his father was dead at the age of seventy-four.[12]

The ensuing stay of three weeks in Germany was another blur. Jünger traveled to Berlin to visit his old friend Carl Schmitt and to find Dahlem in ruins. There he was told that German forces had withdrawn from Tripoli, meaning that combat in North Africa was coming to a close. Judging by his reading on the run (for example, Rimbaud), his thoughts were already turning back to France, though he appropriately found time to finish Gogol's *Dead Souls*, a last farewell gesture to Russia. Paris beckoned again, and on 19 February 1943 a well rehearsed scenario unfolded as Gretha/Perpetua once more sadly parted from her husband at the railroad station in Hanover.[13]

What conclusions may be drawn from the period of less than four months that Ernst Jünger spent in the Soviet Union? The question is easily answered. First, his darkest premonitions were confirmed. All the suspicions and rumors that he had earlier gathered in Paris were patently displayed on the Russian front, so that there needed to be no more conjecture about the bestiality occurring in the East, nor, of course, about the historic advance of mechanization that accompanied it. Second, it became evident that the tide of the war was definitively turning against Germany in both the Russian and North African theaters. These setbacks were almost certainly irreversible and, if so, Jünger was likely to find a far different atmosphere in Paris than he had known during his first tour of duty there. Finally and foremost, he had experienced Russia as the diametric opposite of his gilded life in Paris, as a place where he felt profoundly alien and lacking any real orientation. To reduce this to its ultimate simplicity, Jünger remained a complete stranger in Russia, whereas Paris was his second home. It was altogether fitting, then, that he left Kiev while suffering from a series of acute migraine headaches.

Chapter 6

KNIÉBOLO AND THE NAZIS

One question has until now been largely deferred: what was Ernst Jünger's relationship to National Socialism? The origins of an answer naturally lay deep in Jünger's past and had importantly to do with his fundamental traits as a loner. We saw that he played no part in the uprising of 1918, considering it to be a mutiny rather than a genuine revolution. When the Nazi movement began to emerge soon thereafter, Jünger took a modest personal interest in its strident proclamations of a coming "national dictatorship," for which neither he nor Adolf Hitler's party could provide a clear definition. Some latent enthusiasm was nevertheless evident when Jünger attended a Nazi rally at Munich's Zirkus Krone in 1923 and for the first time listened to the leader in person: "It was not a speech," he later recalled; "it was an elemental happening." But the fiasco of the Beerhall Putsch took place not long thereafter, and Hitler ended in prison, apparently the loser. If Jünger retained a fascination with Hitler, his expectations were henceforth lowered.[1]

In 1925 Jünger briefly joined the Stahlhelm, a veterans' organization that shared his own anti-republicanism, but he rapidly became disaffected and soon disaffiliated. Meanwhile, during his residence in Berlin, he had direct contacts with Joseph Goebbels, a sometime admirer who (like Hitler) had approvingly read Jünger's accounts of trench warfare in France after 1914. But the differences between them became apparent. Jünger remained an elitist, whereas the Nazis appealed to the masses. Jünger favored direct action to force a "true" revolution, whereas the Nazis chose to forgo putschist tactics and to participate in the parliamentary process. Jünger took a dim view of flagrant anti-Semitism, whereas the Nazis exalted it to a central plank of their platform. Hence the contacts with Goebbels and also with Rudolf Hess came to nothing but disillusionment, and arrangements for a meeting between Jünger and the party's Führer were postponed and never realized.[2]

The fact that Jünger declined to join the Nazi Party did not spare him from subsequent criticism that he helped to set the ideological table for Hitler. Such charges cannot be summarily dismissed. Certainly he gave credence to them by his loose references to "blood," "race," and "dictatorship"—evidence of a rhetorical tendency to an extremist nationalism that was at times scarcely distinguishable from the ranting of Nazi fanatics. In a 1930 essay "On Nationalism and the Jewish Question," moreover, he allowed himself some vulgar caricatures of Jews, allegedly guilty of disturbing the purity of the German nation. Still, he continued to disparage fanatical anti-Semites who professed to find a Jew under every rock.[3]

Yet Jünger's support for the Nazi seizure of power in January 1933 was grudging, even though he esteemed Hitler as the gravedigger of the Weimar Republic and perhaps the precursor of greater things to come. He also thought, however, that the Nazi Party was "frumpy" (*spiessig*) and maintained his refusal to join it. When he rejected an offer to be inducted into Berlin's German Academy of Poetry, Goebbels saw to it that no mention of his decision was made in the press. The already chilly relationship between the two thereby found an abrupt end.[4] It was about this time, precisely on 28 April 1939, that Jünger recorded in his journal the first (as it proved) of many dreams about "Kniébolo." It is quite mysterious why he adopted this pseudonym for Hitler, since there could be no question even for a casual reader about Kniébolo's identity. The name was probably derived from "*knebelnder Diabolus*," which might be rendered as "repressive devil." This dream, in any event, portrayed Hitler as a "weak and melancholy" person bent on presenting Jünger with gold-coated candies that he had received in excess for his birthday, barely a week before. As usual, the imagery of this vision cannot be rescued from obscurity, but it is certain that Kniébolo was then and remained thereafter a recurrent figment of Jünger's active imagination.[5]

The beginning of the Second World War launched Jünger into the intense activities previously chronicled and left him little time for dreams and visions. But once he had established residence in the Hotel Raphael in 1941, Kniébolo reappeared, as on 26 June, when Jünger heard of a woman's dream in which the Führer was spied lying on the floor, his face covered with blood.[6] Jünger's waking thoughts were further stirred by a personal assignment, undertaken at the bidding of Hans Speidel, to study the role of the Nazi Party in the military administration of Paris. To this may be added the bizarre fact that Colonel Speidel's son-in-law was the astrologer of Rudolf Hess, leading Jünger to speculate that Hess had flown to England with Kniébolo's permission and was perhaps on a planned mission to solicit a peace accord.[7]

Despite the absence of tape recordings or written evidence, it is safe to assume that the personalities and political machinations of the Third Reich were freely discussed in the tight circle of friends that regularly gathered at the Hotel George V. On occasion, in the Raphael as well, this kind of confidential banter even included some unflattering jokes about the Führer. More seriously, as part of his duties at military headquarters in the Majestic, Jünger continued to gather information about atrocities in Russia and, as mentioned, he was alerted by Speidel about Berlin's darkest intentions concerning the Jews. Frayed nerves were evident during the height of the hostage crisis, when Jünger dreamed of a sea voyage with Kniébolo to the island of Rhodes while the two of them engaged in an unspecified test of wills.[8] In mid-March 1942 Jünger received a visit from Speidel, who shared with him a copy of orders (presumably referring to the roundup of Jews) from Berlin. Jünger took this as proof of Kniébolo's transformation from "*Diabolus*" to "*Satanas*," which may surely be interpreted as a turn for the worse. In general, then, the conclusion seems justified that, during Jünger's first tour in Paris, Kniébolo played the role of a distant yet omnipresent character who represented for him the more sinister and conflictive aspects of the Nazi regime.[9]

Jünger's nearly four months of absence in Russia, when he was preoccupied with vivid scenes of squalor, were a virtual blank insofar as his imaginings of Hitler were concerned. They were marked, we saw, by the end of any illusions about the war, its cruelty, and its probable outcome. Yet Jünger's return to Paris in late February 1943 had all the trappings of a glorious homecoming. After his experiences in Kiev, Rostov, and other Russian towns, the French capital seemed utterly magnificent. Once again he had the run of boulevards, bookstores, parks, cemeteries, and such exquisite restaurants as the Tour d'Argent.[10]

But Jünger's second long stay in the city was not merely a repeat of the first. After the fall of Stalingrad and the bleak news from North Africa, pessimism was rampant in the Occupation and the tone was more sober. Kniébolo was much on his mind. He likened the Führer to Frederick the Great, defending himself from attacks on all sides, but in Kniébolo's case doing so without support or sympathy from others. Jünger's official duties were centered on the oversight of censorship, involving the opening of mail, which he regarded as a difficult and somewhat scurrilous task.[11] Privately, he took up again with Sophie/Charmille and reentered Parisian high society at the salon of Florence Gould and through contacts with various literary personalities like Jean Cocteau and Jean Giraudoux. He made note of the troubling circumstances of men who were twisted by their affections for two women, a matter to which he could personally testify once his wife caught wind of his relationship in Paris with Sophie and made serious remonstrance about it. Perhaps that marital spat was responsible for his occasional migraines and spells of melancholy, although he attempted to persuade himself, despite appearances to the contrary, that "after all everything will improve."[12] Another flash of self-revelation was contained in his reflection that he habitually took more stylistic care when writing to men (such as his brother Friedrich Georg Jünger or Carl Schmitt) than to women, much as a chess player might ration his effort according to the quality of an opponent. As if to test that proposition, Jünger began to participate in regular evening sessions of chess, usually in the Raphael.[13]

Outwardly Paris was somewhat changed. There were noticeably more frequent air raid alarms, and the metro was running irregularly, the familiar green rear-deck buses not at all. Fewer automobiles were circulating in the streets. Bicycles were everywhere. But it was spring, and hundreds could be seen daily promenading under the flowering chestnut trees on the Champs-Élysées.[14] For his part Jünger increased the already hectic pace of social contacts, and there was much name-dropping in his journal: Céline, Cocteau, Valéry, Benoist-Méchin, Bonnard, Giraudoux, Déat—an all-star cast (with the possible exception of Paul Valéry) of collaborators. And then there was Kniébolo. On 16 April 1943 Jünger registered a dream in which Kniébolo visited his father's home. In the dream Jünger withdraws "in order not to meet him." Returning, Jünger finds that Kniébolo had already departed and thus details of the visit must be recounted to him, including his father's embrace of the Führer.[15] Four days later was Hitler's birthday, of which Jünger made no mention but instead elaborated his thoughts of death. Otherwise Jünger took care to create a long paper trail of his observations on Kniébolo. In early May, for example, he became involved in talk about Germany's secret weapons, including ramps for rocket launchings being constructed on the French coast opposite London. The problem was, Jünger remarked, that Kniébolo had always overestimated such novelties.[16] A similar putdown was evident during a discussion with Carl Schmitt at the Hotel Ritz. Even his foes would grant that Hitler possessed "a certain demonic greatness," despite his lack of a Byronic or Napoleonic profile, Jünger remembered saying. Neither photographers nor painters were able to catch his enigmatic face, but his language was mediocre, just as he gathered nullities around him. This did not preclude an acknowledgement of Kniébolo's "elemental overwhelming charisma," which Jünger contrasted to the mere organizational ability of a senior Prussian officer (staying at the Ritz), who was completely without imagination: "This is the reason why [the officer] was and remains incapable of resistance against Kniébolo." From such remarks one may surmise that Jünger's conception of the Nazi leader was both complex and miasmic, a rickety emotional structure of disdain and admiration.[17]

After a four-week furlough in Kirchhorst, Jünger reentered Paris in a foul mood, depressed by the destruction he had seen in German cities along the way and by a report that as many as sixteen thousand persons had been killed in one night of Allied bombing. He deplored "this dreadful escalation of criminality," obviously referring to both sides at once. He also learned of the death in Paris of a young woman who had been "a romantic episode in my life."[18] His consolation were long and lonesome walks in the Bois de Boulogne, where he could hear the distant wailing of air raid sirens to which Parisians had become accustomed. For a time he took up fasting, thus depriving himself of one of the capital's main attractions, and sighed "that the artificial life of this city does not suit me in the long run." He meanwhile reflected on his personal reticence, which he flatteringly attributed to his "absolute love of truth"—hence his halting manner of speaking, since he had to weigh statements against his self-doubts and the criticism of others, whereas they might more easily leap to unsubstantiated conclusions.[19]

This fit of self-analysis was prodded by events beyond Jünger's reach. The news broke of the Allied invasion of Sicily, to which he claimed to respond with stolid indifference, realizing "how much I already stand outside of the national state." The defeat of Nazi Germany seemed to be assured, yet paradoxically, he thought, between East and West "the German position is favorable," which would become more apparent precisely in defeat.[20] In the meanwhile Jünger's attention to the Führer continued. Kniébolo had just commuted the death sentence of a German officer guilty of shooting Russian prisoners because the officer's brother had been murdered by partisans. Jünger commented that Kniébolo wanted a maximum of deaths, a world of corpses, thus the pardon. In this rumination there was undoubtedly a healthy dose of fear. He spent one evening with an officer who had recently sat for twenty minutes opposite Hitler, fascinated by his flashing eyes. The question was then raised: why did Jünger not join the military administration in Berlin? His answer was simply that there he would not have the protection of his friend Heinrich von Stülpnagel. Paris was safer.[21]

On one of Jünger's strolls through the colorful Rue Mouffetard, behind the Pantheon, he regained a feeling of joy and gratitude that this "city of cities" had been spared. This was all the more appropriate at a time when phosphorous bombs were raining onto Hamburg and Hanover, and while the Italian peninsula was becoming the scene of fierce combat. The latter soon led to Mussolini's resignation, noted by Jünger, while the former prompted a story that Germany had possessed such phosphorous munitions during its period of air superiority but had declined to deploy them. If so, Jünger commented, it was a rare and astonishing example of restraint by Kniébolo.[22]

The days of early autumn 1943 passed without major incident. Jünger was nagged by the notion that he was aging: in the staircase of the Majestic he noticed that he was climbing more slowly. He began to read Aldous Huxley. And he continued his therapeutic evening strolls in the Bois de Boulogne, but with a difference. Because many young Frenchmen were now dodging recruitment drives to enlist labor for Germany, the so-called *Service du Travail Obligatoire*, the park was hiding dubious types who were fomenting an atmosphere of lawlessness. Accordingly, Jünger started to carry a pistol when setting out alone. Once back in his room at night he was haunted by dreams of "dreadful anxiety," such as being trapped in purgatory with his father. Likewise, his dreams of writhing snakes recurred with frequency. Little wonder, then, that he repeatedly complained of ill health, loss of weight, and intimations of death.[23]

One episode bears recounting. The air war over France was heating up and it was reaching the Paris region. Some factories in the suburbs, notably Renault, were taking a beating, and a few stray bombs had even fallen in the inner city at the Rue de Rivoli, St.-Placide, and Cherche-Midi. Jünger was fascinated by the spectacle of what seemed to him like a giant display of fireworks. In mid-August he made brief reference to one such instance, which he observed from the roof of the Majestic: the passage overhead of about three hundred planes set off an intense round of anti-aircraft fire. When one of them was hit, he watched as a parachute fluttered down over Montmartre.[24] A similar scenario unfolded a month later. This time Jünger was roused from his room in the Raphael by an air raid siren and hastened to the hotel roof to witness a "frightful and magnificent picture." Two Allied squadrons were flying from northwest to southeast, across the city, leaving clouds of smoke behind and causing Jünger to wonder about "hundreds, perhaps thousands, choked, burning, bleeding." Meanwhile, he could see clearly the silver tails of the bombers against the blue sky, like fishes in water. The roar of their motors sent anxious pigeons shrieking into the air, circling in plain view around the Arch of Triumph. It was for Jünger simultaneously a scene of "great beauty and demonic power." Later, at dusk, he could observe huge fires on the horizon and explosions flashing through the evening sky.[25] For this florid prose and his long-standing tendency to vaunt the aesthetics of warfare, Jünger has been severely taken to task by critics. Whereas, once more, such criticism cannot be lightly waived off, at the same time the reader cannot overlook the author's manifest skill as a writer in creating one of the most eloquent descriptions in his entire journal. Incidentally, after returning to his quarters, Jünger resumed his perusal of Huxley with appreciation for his depiction of sexual ecstasy, and he then dreamed of snakes rearing their heads while beneath them tangled bodies coiled and coupled. There was more fodder for Sigmund Freud, who might have offered that sometimes a snake is just a snake.[26]

During the final months of the year Jünger did not cease to make reference to Kniébolo. Rumors began to arise about plots against the Führer, with which Jünger had no apparent connection. He received the visit of an admirer of his books, Constantin Cramer von Laue, and with him entered into a frank discussion about the extent to which an individual German should bear responsibility for Kniébolo's misdeeds. He read Benoist-Méchin's history of the Prussian army and learned to his delight that Hitler's chauffeur was aptly named Schreck. He listened on the radio to several of Kniébolo's speeches, which reminded him of a bankrupt person at an auction who, in an effort to buy time, assures others that a certain purchase was sure to be extraordinarily profitable. And, in perhaps his most scathing comment on Kniébolo, he wrote that "his biceps are losing their charm."[27]

Jünger spent late November and most of December 1943 in Kirchhorst. He found the sight of a totally flattened Hanover to be depressing, though his sense of impending doom had been even greater when he visited Paris in 1937: "The catastrophe had to occur." That he had actually been so farsighted about the outcome of the war is doubtful, but his additional comment would be worth pondering at any time: we could well guess the future, he wrote, when churches in Russia and synagogues in Germany were forbidden, and when some men, without lawful judgment, forced others into concentration camps.[28]

By Christmas Jünger was back at the Raphael. Heavy bombing of the Paris *banlieue* had virtually become a routine, so that he was greeted by a report that 250 victims had died in a recent air raid. Expectations were that the Allies would invade France within a few weeks. Although that did not prove to be the case, few could doubt that the German Occupation of Paris was entering its ultimate phase or that the next year was bound to bring a decisive military struggle.[29]

(DLA – Marbach)

Jünger leading his troops in the Rue de Rivoli

(ECPA – Ivry-sur-Seine)

Reviewing a motorized unit near the Arch of Triumph

(DLA – Marbach)

Jünger (right) in the Caucasus, 1943

(DLA – Marbach)

Jünger (center) with
Heinrich von Stülpnagel (right)

(DLA – Marbach)

Hans Speidel during the Occupation

(ECPA – Ivry-sur-Seine)

German soldiers at ease on the Place du Tertre

(ECPA – Ivry-sur-Seine)

Military tourists gaining a splendid view of the city

(ECPA – Ivry-sur-Seine)

German army sentinels on the Champs-Élysées

(ECPA – Ivry-sur-Seine)

A show of force at the Place de la Concorde

Chapter 7

THE PLOT AGAINST HITLER

Ernst Jünger began the new year quietly, reflecting on the previous twelve months of 1943 that began for him in Russia and ended back in Paris. His activities were the usual ones: reading (Hölderlin, Alain-Fournier, and Katherine Mansfield's "The Garden Party"); touring the cemeteries of Clichy and Batignolles; strolling through the Latin Quarter, the Rue Mouffetard, and returning to his room in the Raphael. The first anniversary of his father's death was on 9 January, which moved him to read the Book of John in the New Testament and to pass the afternoon in the Church of the Madeleine. He also did not neglect to dream of his father, whom he spotted at a marketplace, standing in a doorway; when soldiers held Jünger back, he and his father winked at each other.[1] Of course, he continued his customary sampling of celebrity salons and fine restaurants, as well as his intimate contacts with Sophie, the Doctoresse. She inspired him to compose a couple of paragraphs on the "eros of intelligence," which he took to be symmetrical like Cupid's bow, a fanciful notion he decided to incorporate into an essay about the relationship of speech and anatomy.[2]

From all of this one might suppose Jünger was effortlessly paddling through the same unruffled waters of his second stint in Paris that he had enjoyed in the first. But times had changed, and he could not avoid facing the reality of what was developing. The worst of his suspicions had been confirmed one evening in the previous October by a visitor in the Hotel Raphael who bore the odd name of "Bogo" (actually a pseudonym for Friedrich Hielscher). Among the things that Bogo recounted were the details of what was occurring in the ghetto of Lodz, now called Litzmannstadt, where an overflowing labor camp was disposing of its huddled excess population by ever more efficient means of extermination. Instead of executions by gunshots to the back of the neck, administered by SS personnel who were thereby psychologically disturbed and sometimes balking, newly arrived Jews who had been deported from German-occupied territories were being herded into gas chambers before their corpses were burned in crematoria. If it was still true in 1944 that many Germans did not know the frightful truth about the mass murder of European Jewry, the same could surely not be said of Ernst Jünger and doubtless of most other officials in occupied Paris. "This is the landscape," Jünger commented, "in which Kniébolo's character is most clearly revealed and which even Dostoyevsky had not foreseen." There was one more matter raised by his guest. An attempt "to blow up Kniébolo" had recently failed, so that this task would henceforth become the assignment of "certain circles." Nothing further was specified in this account of the conversation, but there was no longer room for doubt from this time on that a plot to assassinate Hitler was underway or that Jünger had direct albeit imprecise knowledge of it.[3]

At the outset of 1944 this festering general circumstance took an acutely personal turn for Jünger. News reached him that his elder son, Ernstel, had been arrested for asserting aloud that Hitler deserved to be hanged. Brought to court, the boy showed no remorse, while an informer maintained testimony against him. His guilt was thus a given. Jünger returned at once to Germany in mid-February to plead for Ernstel's release, but in vain. Back in Berlin, he was treated with "slick politeness" by a bureaucratic staff that kept him well away from persons of influence in the military hierarchy. He sought consolation from his old friend Carl Schmitt, who was no longer living at his house in Dahlem, now destroyed, but in a small villa near the Schlachtensee. As Jünger awaited a possible reprieve for Ernstel, he found time to read in Tocqueville's *Democracy in America,* the diaries of Samuel Pepys, André Gide's journals (rather tiresome, he thought), and a volume on China. Even in distress, Jünger remained the consummate dilettante.[4]

By the first week in March, Jünger was again in Paris. After leaving his room in the Raphael one day, he realized that he had forgotten to take his keys with him. He returned to retrieve them and then exited once more onto the Avenue Kléber. It was a common occurrence, he noted, but one that bore out the role of chance in life. His day would be somewhat different because he had left his quarters five minutes later. Here was an example of the trivial yet revealing observations that dotted Jünger's diary, interspersed among more meaningful passages, both of which served to illuminate his self-portrait.[5]

One of those more crucial entries was recorded on 27 March 1944. On that evening Jünger received a visit in his room from Cäsar von Hofacker. Upon entering, Hofacker took the telephone receiver off the hook, evidently a precaution to prevent Gestapo wiretapping. But Hofacker was still uncomfortable; hence the two left the Raphael and went for a long walk, conversing as they paced back and forth between the Trocadéro and the Étoile. Hofacker related that reports by the SS in Paris showed that the circle around Heinrich von Stülpnagel was regarded with the "greatest mistrust" and that Jünger was among those under suspicion. Probably, Hofacker stated, it would be better if Jünger were transferred to Marseille, as he would recommend to the MBF. There is absolutely no question that Hofacker was alluding to a conspiratorial plot against Hitler, or that he was doing so under the under the assumption that Jünger was involved and might support it. Otherwise Hofacker would certainly not have named names, as he did, beginning with Carl Goerdeler, the former Lord Mayor of Leipzig. The Fatherland, he continued, was in grave danger. A catastrophe could no longer be averted, though it might still be mitigated. A collapse in the East would be more calamitous than in the West, and "consequently action must be undertaken in the West" before an Allied cross-channel invasion of the European mainland. "A precondition is the disappearance of Kniébolo," Hofacker said, according to Jünger. The Führer must be eliminated by a bomb, for which the best opportunity would be during a conference at his headquarters in East Prussia.[6]

As Hofacker was in close touch with his cousin, Claus Schenk von Stauffenberg, the man who was to plant that bomb on 20 July 1944, we know that he was well informed about developments in Berlin and that he was now undertaking an initiative to further a simultaneous uprising in Paris. However, insofar as Ernst Jünger was concerned, he was wrong on two fundamental counts: Jünger was not in fact implicated in the conspiracy, and he would not support a plot to neutralize the SS in the French capital. "As already in other similar circumstances," Jünger wrote, "I expressed also here the skepticism, the mistrust, and the reluctance with which the prospect of an assassination attempt fills me." Hofacker nonetheless countered that if Hitler were not stopped, he would take to the radio and within five minutes turn the masses in his favor. Should Heinrich von Stülpnagel throw his full support to the German resistance movement, "on which there is no doubt," other military commanders in the Paris region would fall into line, he claimed. The only problem with that expectation, Jünger could only say, was that Kniébolo's demise would only cause the Nazi hydra to grow new heads.[7]

This story contains several problems and one basic verity. First and most obvious, we have only Jünger's rendition of the exchange with Hofacker, who was arrested immediately after the events of 20 July, mercilessly tortured, and executed. He left no record. Second, a small but telling detail, it seems most unlikely that Hofacker would have referred to Hitler as Kniébolo, as Jünger quoted him. Manifestly, Jünger was putting words into Hofacker's mouth while creating a potentially convenient transcript of his own dissent. That said, the truth is that Jünger had evinced a lifelong disposition to decline support for political movements. Furthermore, Hofacker's revelation that Jünger, as Stülpnagel's personal friend, was suspected by the SS of abetting the conspiracy gave him all the more reason to be cautious: his life was in danger. Without question, both in his dreams and musings, he had expressed distaste and doubt about Hitler such that his attitude must, as usual, be described as ambiguous. Yet the evidence is consistent that Jünger refused his interlocutor's overture to join the resistance and that Hofacker concluded—what else?—Captain Jünger was not to be counted on.

Two days later, on his birthday, Jünger had another delicate conversation, this time with Heinrich von Stülpnagel. Appropriately, there was no mention by either man of Hofacker or Hitler, subjects better avoided. Instead, Jünger was moved to launch into one of his extended sketches of self-evaluation, and in this case it is worth quoting: "Thus I am … a Welf [referring to Hanover], while my notion of the state is Prussian. At the same time I belong to the German nation and am European in my education, indeed a citizen of the world."[8] On that expansive self-congratulatory note he departed once more to visit Gretha in Kirchhorst in a second attempt to rescue Ernstel from prison. It was important that his son be freed, he said, "before the catastrophe." For that purpose Jünger traveled to Wilhelmshaven on the North Sea, where Ernstel was incarcerated and where the boy seemed pale and sickly. He was soon to be released.[9]

Once returned to Paris in late April, Jünger found more signs of impending doom. There were frequent airplanes overhead, sirens screaming, and a distant sight of bombing behind Montmartre and in the adjacent northern suburb of St.-Denis. Next to the Raphael a huge ugly concrete bunker had been erected, to which hotel residents were supposed to flee during an alarm. Jünger preferred to remain in bed, though he was aware that casualties throughout the Paris area could now be counted in the hundreds. Several sections of the city, such as the Place des Invalides, had been cordoned off to create anti-aircraft stations.[10] In the meanwhile Jünger caught up with recent events through talks with Hans Speidel, who had become General Erwin Rommel's new chief of staff. They met at Rommel's headquarters in a castle farther down the Seine, 80 kilometers due west, at La Roche-Guyon. Jünger also found occasion for further chats with Heinrich von Stülpnagel, who confided his worries that General Gerd von Rundstedt's reservations were preventing clarity about the situation, that is, "an unmasking." Presumably this was a barely disguised allusion to the plot that was continuing to coalesce, though it was unsure how firm either's support for it would be. Jünger had reason to believe that the MBF was at least sympathetic to "the Fronde" of resisters. But vice versa?[11]

On 8 May Jünger entertained a visit from Clemens Podewils, who had recently accompanied Rommel on an inspection of the Atlantic Wall. Everyone, it seemed, was expecting a series of imminent Allied landings, and Rommel wanted to meet them on the beaches. The question was when and where. Jünger's opinion was that Great Britain would be better served by holding off an invasion of the mainland and allowing the sapping conflict between Germany and Russia to continue in the East. It was unlikely, in any event, that the two great powers would conclude a deal, as in the First World War, because Kniébolo would forbid it. Thus Hitler, in effect, was the mortar holding the anti-German coalition together. "The situation is not yet desperate for Germany," Jünger ventured, "but what disgust it brings to watch this spectacle."[12] Others were perhaps not so revolted, but they were often less optimistic. When he again visited La Roche-Guyon to see Hans Speidel, whom he more and more admired and in fact considered "the decisive man" on the German side, he heard his friend put the situation into categorical terms: "By autumn the war in Europe will be at an end." Fittingly, Jünger began to read about "the great destruction" in the Book of Revelation.[13]

It would be remiss here to omit mention of another of Jünger's aesthetic thrills as he watched the unfolding air war over Paris from the rooftop terrace of the Hotel Raphael. On this occasion in late May, he witnessed a pair of explosions in the direction of the Boulevard St.-Germain. His assumption was that they resulted from a bombing of bridges over the Seine. But there must have been some other explanation, since it is well known that American and RAF pilots had strict instructions not to attack the inner city of Paris. Whatever the case, Jünger could not suppress his delight at seeing this brilliant display at sundown as he held in his hand a glass of Burgundy wine with floating strawberries in it. Before him, as he wrote, "with its red towers and domes, the city lay in majestic beauty." The preciousness of this scene could not fail to elicit howls of protest from Jünger's critics after the war, and it seems only fair to judge that he did in this instance allow himself one emotional binge too many.[14]

On the last day of May Jünger once more traveled to Vaux-les-Cernay to see "the blond Stülpnagel." Jünger was one of the many to admire Heinrich's calmness and elegance, as well as his broad knowledge of mathematics, his grasp of philosophy, and his love of Byzantine history. These "princely traits" helped to explain the MBF's aversion to Kniébolo. "But he is tired," Jünger observed, thereby accurately characterizing the General's relationship to the planning for an uprising in Paris that would accompany an attempt on Hitler's life. Stülpnagel would passively support it, if successful, but he was by no means its driving force.[15]

In early June Jünger again spent an evening with Speidel at La Roche-Guyon. Because he did not return to the Raphael until after midnight and slept late, he missed the first reports of the Normandy landings.[16] He was not alone to be surprised. Rommel himself was absent altogether, having departed to Germany to visit his wife on her birthday. Key actors were not always at the ready when it came time for action. Famously, Rommel was to be removed from activity in July after he was injured when an Allied bomb struck his vehicle. It is thus impossible to determine how much difference the full participation in the plot against Hitler by individuals like Stülpnagel and Rommel would have made in the final outcome. The same may be said of "the so-called new weapon" allegedly possessed by the Führer, a topic often discussed in Paris salons. Jünger was unimpressed with such rumors, arguing that if Germany really possessed more effective weapons, they would have been deployed against the Allied beachheads in Normandy. That failing, they amounted to nothing but propaganda.[17]

Jünger was fully aware that something was afoot in Paris. On 17 June 1944 he received a visit in his room at the Raphael from Lieutenant Heinrich von Trott zu Solz, whose brother Adam had long been an active conspirator against Hitler. Their conversation turned to the prospect of "great events" on the horizon. Nothing further was specified, at least not in Jünger's journal, but the steady accumulation of evidence over the past several months, notably including his frank talks with Cäsar von Hofacker, could have left no doubt about Trott's intended inference.[18] Jünger learned more detail from another trip in late June to La Roche-Guyon, where he conferred with Speidel, who had recently met in Soissons with the Führer to file a report in person. Hitler looked worn and stooped, Jünger recalled Speidel saying, and he was apparently under heavy medication. The Führer had no clear idea of how the combat was likely to develop, Speidel disclosed, but he twice invoked the precedent of the Seven Years War and boasted of "unknown new weapons" that would be unleashed in the autumn. Jünger's apprehensions were only increased. On the last night of the month he dreamed about the Oberförster, that evil marauding commander in his fantasy novel *Auf den Marmorklippen*. Although in his dream Jünger carried a weapon to the encounter, he was helpless to react against the other's charismatic aura.[19]

By mid-July the Russians had invaded East Prussia and the Americans were in Florence. Both sides were suffering heavy casualties in Normandy, where the Allies were attempting to break out from the peninsula. Meanwhile "the [German] leadership is attempting to raise hopes of the people for new weapons," Jünger wrote with skepticism, "because it is incapable of new ideas."[20] From Speidel, who was frequently on the phone with Hitler, Jünger gathered more hints of the approaching storm. Confidentially, of course, they speculated together about "how much time the Germans will still need to rid themselves of this shooting-gallery figure." The attempt to do so, we know, was only a matter of hours away. As if to relieve the tension, or perhaps just to avoid the issue, Jünger joined Clemens Podewils on a tour of Claude Monet's garden at Giverny.[21]

Ernst Jünger played no part in the dramatic events of 20 July 1944. That day he lunched in the Hotel Raphael with Heinrich von Stülpnagel and two other officers before withdrawing at 2 PM to spend the afternoon in the Bois de Boulogne, well out of the way. About 4 PM the first report arrived at military headquarters in the Majestic about the attempt on Hitler's life, and it was confidently rumored that the Führer was dead and that his assassin, Colonel von Stauffenberg, was in charge at the Bendlerstrasse in Berlin. While, as we know, Operation Walküre was soon to collapse in Germany once it became certain that Hitler had survived, the simultaneous insurrection in Paris initially succeeded. More than a thousand SS and security police agents were summarily arrested, and the MBF temporarily assumed command of occupied France.[22] Heinrich von Stülpnagel, who had spent the afternoon in La Roche-Guyon, meanwhile returned to Paris, where he was promptly confronted with the latest news from Berlin and called onto the carpet of the officers' casino in the Hotel Raphael. Shortly after midnight German Ambassador Otto Abetz appeared, as did SS-chief Carl Oberg, who had just been released from confinement in the Hotel Continental. A bizarre scene ensued as these strange bedfellows, after shaking hands, joined in a general champagne-lubricated revelry. Soon informed of his dismissal as MBF, Stülpnagel retired to his quarters in the Raphael about 4 AM and awaited the dawn.[23]

Ernst Jünger's exact whereabouts in Paris during these crucial hours were, and remain, unknown. He simply made note on the next day of "the highly dangerous situation." He was personally unacquainted with Hitler's would-be assassin, "a Count Stauffenberg ... whose name I have heard from Hofacker." Correctly, he feared that the coming retributions for the plot would turn into a slaughter. And he had reason to believe, despite his refusal to resort to intrigue, that his name might appear on the list of potential victims. Yet he drew a lesson from the *Marmorklippen*: "I have for a long time been convinced that through assassination attempts little will be changed and, above all, nothing improved."[24]

At nine o'clock on the morning of 21 July, Stülpnagel received orders to return to Berlin. He prepared to leave, choosing to travel by auto rather than airplane. He bade farewell to his staff in the Hotel Majestic about 11 AM but remembered that he was scheduled to have breakfast in the Raphael with Ernst Jünger. Turning to his secretary, he said: "I am sorry that it is no longer possible. But greet Captain Jünger cordially for me and inform him of my trip to Berlin." These were Heinrich von Stülpnagel's last words as he strode through the front door of the Hotel Majestic, stepped into his waiting limousine in the Avenue Kléber, and sped off toward Germany.[25]

The rest of the story has often been recounted. Arriving en route at Verdun, where he had served during the First World War, Stülpnagel stopped his car, wandered off, and then attempted suicide by a pistol shot to his temple, but managed only to blind himself. Taken to Berlin, he was given a mock trial, condemned, and hanged by a thin wire from a meat hook. Of all this, and more, Jünger wrote only a brief passage of regret for the sacrifice of "the last knightly humans" who had by their deed prevented the entire German nation from falling as a block into "the terrible depths of fate." Such literary flourish must seem feeble indeed as a personal tribute to Heinrich von Stülpnagel and to the dozens of others who perished in an effort to save a vestige of German honor.[26]

An explanation, or excuse, for Jünger's comportment in July 1944 is difficult to formulate. His habitual stance as an outsider was surely relevant. Also his recollection of the *Marmorklippen*, his most acclaimed novel, was a significant clue to his mind-set: as ever, he was true not to a cause but to self. And that self knew fear. Baldly to accuse Jünger of cowardice would be cheap, especially on the part of a critic who has not known the kind of tragic and threatening circumstances Jünger faced. Yet fear was unquestionably a factor, an emotion known after 1939 to millions of Europeans who were forced to live and attempt to survive under Nazi domination. Kniébolo ruled absolutely, and it is no wonder that others quaked in his presence. There was another factor that naturally found no place in Jünger's account. Apparently, the truth was that the conspirators did not fully trust him. During his long walk and intense exchange with Cäsar von Hofacker in the previous March, it was obvious that he was being sounded out as a possible fellow conspirator. Since we do not have any record of the occasion by Hofacker, that surmise cannot be confirmed. Yet it is most likely, even based on Jünger's own testimony. If so, the following supposition by one of Jünger's biographers must be regarded as quite implausible: "As an accomplice he did not come into question for the conspirators, since, as a still famous author who might play a leading intellectual role after a successful overthrow, [Jünger] was too important to have his life risked in the action."[27] Too important? More important than Stauffenberg, or Hofacker, or Heinrich von Stülpnagel, among many others? No conclusion could be more dubious.

The end came very quickly. After the Allied breakout from Normandy in late July, Paris was besieged. Orders were issued for the military administration in the capital to evacuate to eastern France. An atmosphere of panic ran through the Raphael. Jünger enjoyed a parting breakfast with Sophie, his Paris love, and bade farewell to several others, including his barber, who spoke these last words: "*J'espère que les choses s'arrangeront.*" Of course they would not.[28] Jünger also found time for a final climb up to Montmartre, where he looked out over Paris from the steps in front of Sacré Coeur. "Cities are feminine," he wrote as an epitaph, "and are only faithful to the victor."[29] After tidying his room in the Raphael and leaving flowers and a tip for the hotel staff, he departed for Lorraine. Once arrived there, he dreamed of standing on marble steps covered with snakes attempting to slither upward. Soon after the news reached Jünger that the Americans had entered the French capital, he dreamed of strolling through a wonderful and elegant city. But once back with Gretha in Kirchhorst, by September, he well knew that in reality his marvelous days and nights in Paris were at an end.[30]

Chapter 8

TELLING OMISSIONS

In retrospect it is clear that Ernst Jünger's journals are of interest not only for what they tell us about the German occupation of Paris but for what they do not. Just as he had sanitized his memoirs of the First World War through many successive revisions of the original text, so he proceeded likewise with his later journals as he moved from notes and jottings to drafts and then to publications. The final result was a highly stylized account of his experience, not a literal record but a literary recreation of his dual role as actor and author. Thus Jünger did not offer a documentary chronicle of events but attempted to convey his abiding impression of them. Although his journals therefore often lacked immediacy, nonetheless they cannot be classified as fiction—not even, as one critic has contended, when they read rather like a bildungsroman.[1]

Manifestly, more than a few problems of interpretation arise because of Jünger's tendency to dehistoricize his prose, that is, to omit or deliberately to dissimulate certain facts and identities in the ultimate printed version of his journals. Scholars who have carefully examined earlier notes and drafts on which the journals are based have uncovered a number of such omissions.[2] It cannot be said that the discovery of these deletions has basically altered the essential narrative of Jünger's wartime writings or revealed hitherto unsuspected facets of his personality. Yet it is worthwhile to summarize these findings in order to probe more deeply into Jünger's rendition of the Paris years. To lend this analysis some structure and coherence it will be useful to consider four signal categories of omission, each of which indicates a principal aspect of

Jünger's activities under the Occupation that received little or no mention in his published journals.

Sex: Surely it is not surprising that Captain Jünger chose to tone down the more intimate scenes of his love life (nor, of course, was he alone among diarists to do so). If he was not quite a Casanova, he certainly had plenty of occasions to boast about an amorous adventure. Yet, except for the one incident cited earlier when he met a girl at the Place des Ternes and then fondled her bosom in a Paris cinema, he avoided any graphic descriptions of his many contacts with French women. Instead, the reader is soon lost in a maze of evasions, faint allusions, and false identities.

As noted, Jünger had his reasons. He obviously felt both a need to protect the security of those with whom he had liaisons and to guard his own reputation, as well as to salvage his marriage once his wife discovered the truth about his philandering behavior. These understandable motives came particularly into play in regard to Sophie Ravoux, unquestionably his most constant and significant female companion in Paris. Comparison of Jünger's drafts with his published texts leaves not the slightest question that he repeatedly crossed out her name and substituted one of several *Decknamen* that he attributed to her. It was perhaps she, under the pseudonym of "Dorothea," who touched Jünger's body with her long fingers; she with whom he passed a cozy night, undoubtedly one among many; she with whom he strolled one evening to the Square du Vert-Galant on the Seine without later recording what followed; she who appeared again and again as "the Doctoresse" while being escorted by Jünger to the theater or some fancy soirée; and so on. There were other instances of hidden identity, interestingly including that of Florence Gould, who on occasion turns up as "Lady Orpington," leading at least one historian to speculate that Jünger also had an affair with her. On this matter, needless to add, he remained silent.[3]

Related, though without sexual implications, was Jünger's frequent use of pseudonyms for contemporaries whom he wanted either to caricature or protect. For instance, besides Hitler's ubiquitous "Kniébolo," there was Heinrich Himmler as "Schinderhannes," Goebbels as "Grandgoschier," the imprisoned Ernst Niekisch appropriately named "Cellaris," and "Bogo" (or "Bodo") for Friedrich Hielscher. Many of these monikers seem to have been selected for Jünger's amusement, often presumably to express his distance from the individual in question. Above all, however, it was the detail of his erotic escapades and intimate evenings that Jünger decided to suppress, preferring to cloak them in a cloud of generalities or misleading identifications.[4]

Common people: Although Jünger has been justifiably praised by some authors for his evocation of Paris under the Occupation, as a rule his view was in fact limited to certain strata of Parisian life. He circulated freely and perceptively in the salons of high society, a wide circle of French artists and intellectuals, and the comradely gatherings of fellow German officers. Yet one finds in his journals remarkably little reference to daily life of the populace in Paris, to street scenes, bread lines, or chats with *bouquinistes* and fishermen along the Seine. Symptomatically, Jünger was taken aback one day in August 1942 by the hateful stare of a Parisian shop girl, as if he scarcely realized the animosity aroused among ordinary people by the presence of an occupying foreign army.[5] The resulting picture of Paris was thus subjectively distorted to some extent, either by aesthetics or omissions. Jünger seems to slouch through the city, imperturbable, protected by a thick emotional carapace that enabled him to maintain his habitual aloofness. His journals thereby suggest narcissism comprised of irony, simple elegance, and a solid conviction of intellectual superiority.

Often Jünger has been more harshly chastised for what he did not include in his journals than for what he did. There is no suffering. People disappear or die, but they do not anguish. The journals report incidents of bombings in the Paris region and the estimates of those killed. Yet this is always a view from the largely untouched inner city, from the rooftop of the Raphael, conveying no sense of destruction in the suburbs. Rather, as we saw, Jünger indulged his penchant for aesthetic portrayals of episodes such as the infamous strawberries-in-wine scene that has enraged more than one critic.[6]

Surprisingly little was said in the journals about Jews. True, Jünger did not fail to enter his feelings of shame upon seeing yellow stars for the first time on the streets of Paris. But he hardly mentioned the mass deportations that began in 1942, nor did he appear to lament the hundreds of executions occurring at Mont Valérien on the eastern edge of the capital, a fact known even when not directly witnessed by all German officers and many Parisians. The term "concentration camp" was not part of Jünger's vocabulary. He resorted instead to another term, "*Schinderhütte,*" adopted from his fictional *Auf den Marmorklippen,* which had the effect of transposing the horror of current history from the realm of reality to an imaginary land of parable. It followed that Jünger nowhere referred directly to Auschwitz at a time when thousands of French Jews were being sent there to a certain death. To be sure, Jünger made no attempt to justify mass murder, but neither would he clearly denounce it.[7]

Condemnation: Here is the characteristic of Jünger's journals most delicate and difficult to define. To begin with, although he stoutly guarded a healthy skepticism toward Hitler and the Nazi Party, he did so within a framework of historical relativism. In this perspective Stalin could be seen as a counterpart and perhaps even a forerunner of Hitler—a proposition that came uncomfortably close to foreshadowing an assertion that sparked the so-called *Historikerstreit* of the 1980s in which the German scholar Ernst Nolte was reprimanded by several of his colleagues for making much the same argument.[8] Hence, for Jünger Nazi terror might be thought comparable to the bombing of Dresden or to the violence that occurred at war's end during the Russian invasion of Eastern Europe and Germany. Moreover, the war and the undeniable atrocities that ensued from it could be cast by Jünger as part of a vast historical development, under the guise of modernity, and therefore as a phenomenon not directly caused by individuals or nations. If so, in this great march of metahistory, no one could fairly be charged—whatever the brutality or stupidity—with personal responsibility for individual actions in this huge predestined scenario.

Jünger's indulgent portrayal of the cousins Otto and Heinrich von Stülpnagel can best be evaluated in this light. As MBF, commander of the German army in occupied France, Otto von Stülpnagel emerged in Jünger's published recounting as a tragic figure caught in an impossible circumstance. The hostage crisis was not of his making, and he nobly attempted on moral principles to stem the tide of it. But close examination of Jünger's rough drafts has disclosed that Otto in fact denied that he acted solely on moral grounds; rather, his reasons were political, his actions taken in order to assure a smooth and orderly military administration. After all, he approved the execution of dozens of French hostages, ordinarily designated as Jews or Communists, and he recommended that persons rounded up in what were euphemistically called "atonement measures" (*Sühnemassnahmen*) should be sent off to camps "in the East," an obvious code for extermination. When Otto suffered a nervous breakdown and was replaced by Heinrich von Stülpnagel, the latter's more chivalrous demeanor, much admired by Jünger, did not hide the fact that he actually perpetuated the same policy.[9]

On balance, then, the version of events offered in Ernst Jünger's *Pariser Tagebücher* can scarcely be considered an accurate retelling of the persons and policies involved in the German administration of occupied Paris. Crucial details omitted from it create the misleading impression that the army and its leaders in Paris were "clean" and that they consistently struggled to offset the fanaticism of Nazi Party regulars, SS henchmen, and secret police. If Jünger intended thereby to exonerate the two Stülpnagels and their military coterie, he failed to outwit the diligent researchers who have labored in the archival vineyards to uncover the inner workings of the military regime in Paris.[10]

One addendum in this regard may be allowed. Jünger's presentation of the Paris years certainly derived in large measure from his earlier career. It is true that, as a young man, he favored a "conservative revolution" but refused to pledge allegiance to Nazism. The problem was that he made a sufficient analysis of neither. He carefully avoided using the term National Socialism, preferring to write with vague references to nihilism. Yet it was never clear what form a nihilistic revolution could take. In general, therefore, fascism could be understood by Jünger as just another radical theory of plebiscitary democracy, and Nazism could be presented not as a perversion of it for which the German nation was responsible but merely as the symptom of some European moral crisis in the twentieth century. Hence it was altogether logical that Jünger should end by rejecting any notion of a collective German guilt.[11]

Commitment: Many memoirs and autobiographies attempt to explain how their authors devoted their lives to one cause or another, a laudable endeavor with which they closely identified themselves and for which they then bravely sacrificed. Decidedly, such an element is lacking in Ernst Jünger's journals. One misses any sense of deep commitment, whether to a movement, to a party, or to persons—including his spouse and his favorite lover in Paris. His initial reluctance and final refusal to join with the conspirators of 20 July 1944 in Paris were thus perfectly in character for him, as was his almost casual acceptance of the plot's failure and the tragic end of his erstwhile friend Heinrich von Stülpnagel. Accordingly, it appears that Jünger's self-asserted *désinvolture* tended to be virtually synonymous with insouciance toward nearly everything and everyone, a tenuous attachment to this world and those who inhabit it. "This," as one of his critics has accurately but somewhat too archly put it, "enables him to wander with impunity close to the fires of evil and yet never to fall under their hypnotic power. In the world of human passions he has no capacity for kinship, not even with himself."[12]

Still, Jünger at least had the virtue of his faults. If he rarely displayed a close relationship to others, he was also a man of few prejudices. He was obviously a person with great curiosity about nature and the human condition, both of which he observed with care and attention to detail. Jünger's innate reticence to move from disinterested observation to genuine commitment commendably saved him from being swept into the excesses of Nazism. To his credit, he consistently disapproved of zealous anti-Semitism, and he maintained a circumspect detachment from Adolf Hitler and his most devoted acolytes.

The only important exception to his noncommittal comportment was arguably the army, to which he remained faithful throughout the second Thirty Years War from 1914 to 1945. Although his military duties during the Paris years undoubtedly concerned him far less than his contacts with German colleagues and French intellectuals, he nevertheless remained a military man, an officer comfortable on horseback at the head of his trailing troops. At no time did he seriously question the role of the German army in the Second World War or challenge the legitimacy of the Occupation in France. Hence, whereas he felt free to criticize the conduct of military and political affairs of the Third Reich, he did not deny the necessity of the conflict in which he was engaged. In later years Jünger commented on his own passivity while stationed in Paris: "I did my duty conscientiously there, however without great passion and without distinguishing myself. ... I never advanced beyond the rank of captain and accomplished nothing exceptional."[13]

For all these reasons it is dubious to classify Ernst Jünger as a proto-fascist or to dismiss him as a foot soldier of the far right in Nazi Germany. Unfailingly, he displayed a complexity that defies easy labeling. Unsatisfactory as it may seem, the word that still most readily comes to mind when attempting to summarize Jünger's life and his journals is ambiguity.

Chapter 9

Immediate Afterthoughts

In August 1944 Ernst Jünger left Paris, but Paris never left him. The city remained in his thoughts, in his dreams, in his imagination, and in his literary works. It seemed almost as if Kirchhorst were an exile for him. In the first weeks after leaving Paris there was little to occupy his attention. Soon mustered out of the army, he assumed duties—such as they were—as the commander of a local militia unit (*Volkssturm*). But Jünger knew war, and he realized that Germany's military position was hopeless. Hence he was thoroughly convinced that erecting barriers against American tanks was useless effort. Jünger tried to keep up with the news. He learned in mid-August that Paris, in defiance of Kniébolo's orders, had been spared by the German army of occupation, for which General Dietrich von Choltitz and Hans Speidel were to thank. A week later the Americans entered Paris. Reports from France came in bits and scraps: Drieu la Rochelle shot himself; Henry de Montherlant was being pursued; Jacques Benoist-Méchin was executed by "terrorists"; Jünger's friend Speidel was arrested (and later released).[1] His health seemed to be faltering, causing him to spend many hours in bed, perchance to dream. As so often before, his father returned to him in his sleep, and memories of Paris recurred, such as visiting Paul Verlaine's gravesite, touring the cemetery of Batignolles, or gathering with others at the salon of Florence Gould: "There I was again in Paris." He also dreamed of Heinrich von Stülpnagel, seeing him alive and concluding that reports of his death might be false; but he could not shrink from the sight of a scar from a gunshot wound on the General's temple.[2]

The war continued to close in. There was fighting in Holland, Alsace, and East Prussia, as well as Poland, Hungary, Czechoslovakia, Italy, Greece, and the Balkans. His elder son Ernstel, once freed from prison, had enlisted in the army and was sent to Italy. Unknown to Jünger until six weeks after the fact, Ernstel fell in battle on 29 November, soon after seeing his first combat. "Ernstel is dead," he wrote simply on 12 January 1945, a blow from which he would never recover. It was like "a wound that will not heal." Once again the single appropriate word for him was "*Schmerz,*" a relentless pain like a rain soaking in, only becoming wetter and worse with time.³ This morose tone crowded out everything else for a while. He nonetheless recorded events as they occurred: the first snowfall of winter; the show trials of the 20 July 1944 conspirators in Berlin; the passage of hundreds of Allied bombers; false rumors that he himself had been arrested or killed; an incident when two American pilots, after their parachutes became entangled, had fallen nearby to their death (Jünger visited their graves); the news that the "old and beautiful" city of Freiburg had been utterly destroyed in one night within twenty minutes.⁴

At the end of 1944 Jünger's existence was severely limited. Travel was nearly impossible, except for local excursions on a bicycle. Even that was difficult. Munitions had fallen near Kirchhorst, some of them time bombs yet to explode. He did visit Hanover briefly, finding the city—his city—in ruins and flames. While there he retraced his old pathway to school (before the First World War), along which there had once been many shop windows overflowing with goods for sale. They were no more. He stopped at a "spiritual place" that reminded him of the Place des Ternes in Paris.⁵ And he received a visit from Cramer von Laue, whom he had known there and who, after being wounded in Italy, was now on crutches. They spoke of the 20 July plot and agreed that, despite his survival, Kniébolo's health had suffered badly from the attack. There could be no doubt that the Führer's days were numbered. It was altogether fitting that Jünger began reading a series of books about shipwrecks.⁶

As customary, Jünger quietly observed the anniversary of his father's death on 9 January 1945. He learned of Ernstel's end only three days later, and he thereupon combined grief for his father and his son. This gloom was deepened by news of the total destruction of Dresden, causing Jünger to expound on the demerits of an early success. After the fall of France in 1940, there had been great jubilation in Germany, where the voices of the unfortunate losers went unheard. Reason had been swept away by power. Now Germany was suffering the consequences. Allied bombing was made all the more dreadful by the severe cold of winter, and "death has now approached so near."⁷ Soon thereafter Jünger recorded another dream sequence in which he was busily preparing a conference room for a meeting with the English about the use of poison gas. Kniébolo appeared, and Jünger remarked that "for him every death, no matter how many on which side, was a gain."⁸ In the meantime, Allied troops were entering Limburg, Giessen, Aschaffenburg, and Frankfurt. According to Jünger, given to misplaced relativism, "the situation of the Germans is now exactly as it was for the Jews inside Germany."[9]

On 29 March 1945 *Volkssturmführer* Ernst Jünger celebrated his fiftieth birthday, which marked for him "the middle of life", a notion more literally true than he could then have realized (he lived to be nearly 103 years old).[10] The elderly men and young boys under his command were digging trenches, though it was unclear for what purpose. The Americans were in Paderborn, the English on the Weser, not far away. Refugees were streaming this way and that, some eastward and some westward. On 10 July two American tanks rolled into Kirchhorst, which officially capitulated on the next day. For Captain Jünger, not alone, the war was blessedly over.[11]

In the immediate postwar years much was different. For one thing, at last, Kniébolo disappeared from Jünger's journals. When newspaper accounts reached him of Mussolini's death, he also heard rumors about "Hitler." And on the first day of May 1945 he heard an announcement of "Hitler's" death by poison in Berlin. This report, he noted, did not quite accord with the picture he recalled from 1942 when, while in Paris at the Café de la Paix, he was told about a vision of the Führer's face covered with blood. At least the Kniébolo of that time was gone.[12] Jünger also remembered speaking with a French acquaintance in Paris about a parallel between Hitler and General Georges Boulanger (an aspiring political leader of the late nineteenth century), both of whom ended their lives with a suicide. But the implied comparison between the French Third Republic and the Weimar Republic in Germany was admittedly wanting, and the analogy went no further in Jünger's writings.[13]

For the first time in years there were no more nightly blackouts in Germany. Yet there was censorship, and Jünger was under constraint, prohibited by the British authorities in their northern zone of occupation to publish. Naturally he thought back to his days in the Majestic when opening and censoring letters was one of his principal official duties. In retrospect he was not proud of that service rendered. But, quite characteristically, he remarked that all things in life cannot be totally just: "One can only act approximately, more or less right, more or less wrong."[14] Such recollections of Paris were also stirred by an encounter with two American journalists, Jünger's first human contact with the other side in six years (since he did not count the French as enemies). Besides stopping in Paris, they had recently made a tour of a concentration camp "in the vicinity of Weimar." Apparently Jünger did not recognize the name of Buchenwald, to which this was an obvious reference. Instead, he passed on to write a brief essay about one of his favorite themes, the progressive mechanization of modern life, evident in the more efficient killings of his time as compared to the guillotine during the French Revolution, model scenes of which he had seen at the Musée Carnavalet in the Paris Marais. Speaking of

Americans, it may be appended that Jünger's view of their hapless vulgarity was still intact, as when he remarked that it would be a shame to waste a glass of Burgundy wine on "people from Kentucky."[15]

Another interesting aside was Jünger's reaction to a report that the captured Heinrich Himmler had committed suicide by swallowing a cyanide capsule hidden under his tongue. What had always struck him about Himmler, he wrote, was how "penetratingly bourgeois" he was. Without elaborating at length, Jünger thereby unwittingly expressed a tentative version of a view quite similar to Hannah Arendt's much later and more highly expanded thesis about the banality of evil.[16]

Paris was brought to Jünger's attention both by his reading and by occasional guests. As in the past, he spent an inordinate amount of time poring over the works of Léon Bloy, recently including *Le Salut par les Juifs* and *Mon Journal*. He also plunged into Balzac, an author whom he now appreciated more than ever because his mind's eye was able to recognize many of the mentioned streets and squares in Paris.[17] Meanwhile, in June 1945, he entertained his old friend Martin von Katte. They spoke of the attempt on Hitler's life nearly a year before and made comparisons with the assassination of the Bavarian Prime Minister Kurt Eisner in 1919. This discussion led Jünger to repeat his earlier observations that assassination attempts generally provide false solutions, since "they raise problems to another [but] no better level."[18] A second visitor with memories of the recent past was Colonel Ernst Schaer, who had been one of Jünger's colleagues in the Hotel Majestic. Schaer was demoted and briefly imprisoned in 1941 for criticizing the leadership of the Nazi Party after the invasion of Russia. Jünger had helped him to gain release and protection from Heinrich von Stülpnagel. In the wake of the 20 July plot, however, he was once more arrested and incarcerated in Paris before being spared by General von Choltitz. Thus he lived to tell his tale. Jünger and he had much to talk about. In fact, as they thought back together to their Paris days, "some things gradually become clearer." For instance, they subsequently found out that the German security police succeeded in planting an agent in the Raphael, a French room clerk who reported to Gestapo headquarters in the Avenue Foch. No one had suspected that he understood German.[19]

In August Jünger recollected conversations in the Raphael and the Hotel George V about whether there was any way at some point during the war to avert or at least to mitigate a catastrophe. Jünger's considered opinion, then and now, was a flat negative. Rather, it had been as if they were sitting on a speeding train that was moving faster and faster, making any attempt to jump from it increasingly hopeless and suicidal. Among military officers housed at the Raphael, at least those known to Jünger, the legal comportment of the Third Reich was most harshly criticized. But the Allied doctrine of unconditional surrender, announced by Franklin D. Roosevelt and Winston Churchill at the Casablanca Conference in January 1943, had made Clausewitz obsolete and a compromise impossible. Although such a critique of Anglo-American wartime policy was common currency in postwar Germany, it has to be said that Jünger's analysis of it left much to be desired, namely an equally unequivocal condemnation of Nazi ideology and aggression.[20]

Jünger spent much time in late 1945 ordering his papers. While doing so, he became aware of how many lacunae were left, because in Paris, in a fit of nervousness, he had burned evidence that might be compromising for himself or others. These expurgated files notably included those of both Heinrich von Stülpnagel and Cäsar von Hofacker, thus depriving historians of valuable documents that might have better illuminated Jünger's role in the Occupation and the 20 July 1944 plot. He especially regretted the absence of his correspondence with Stülpnagel, of which he retained nothing but a few notes concerning their mutual interest in botany. It was unfortunate, he commented, that Heinrich's predecessor as MBF in Paris was also named Stülpnagel, since the change of regime in February 1942 was hardly noticed by the French, even though the two men embodied distinctly different personalities. Otto was simply not suited for the crucial position he held. He loved to wear his uniform with shiny leather boots and gold buttons, which behind his back earned him the sobriquet of "King Nutcracker." He was at once lovable and nervous, incapable of standing up to the perpetual quarreling of factions in Paris or the German military authority in France (called OB West) represented at first by General von Rundstedt and then by General Günther von Kluge. Especially troublesome and unmanageable for the MBF was the Gestapo, which independently staged arrests and razzias, roundups and deportation of Jews, and the enforced wearing of the yellow Star of David—all of which was incompatible with an orderly administration of the Occupation in Paris. Finally there was the hostage crisis, as Jünger remembered it, a series of retributions commanded by Berlin after the murder of a few German officials. Suffering a nervous breakdown as a consequence, Otto von Stülpnagel submitted his resignation, to be replaced by his calmer, more elegant, but not remarkably more effective cousin.[21]

After the first rush of events at the war's end, Jünger's journal entries became sparser and less revealing. He recorded little of note during the first half of 1946 and nothing at all for the rest of that year. He did begin to develop a new theme about what he entitled "Provocation and Response." In 1918–1919, for example, Germany was provoked by the Versailles Treaty and Hitler was the response. The Führer in turn became a provocation to which the war was a response. But the banality of this historical construction, at best a sort of insipid Hegelianism, must have become all too apparent, and he dropped it altogether.[22] Arguably, his most eloquent and prescient passages concerned the possible future of a European union, which he considered a matter of life or death for Germany and also for France and other smaller states. As he correctly noted: "The Second World War brought frightful destruction, but it also weakened prejudices that seemed irrepressible and forced open doors that can no longer be closed." Jünger would live to see his prophecy amply fulfilled. Whether his contacts with French intellectuals during the Paris years had anything to do with furthering that end, as he imagined, may be doubtful. Yet surely the period of the German Occupation, in which he took part, should not be detached from any analysis of the unprecedented reconciliation of European nations after 1945.[23]

Although Jünger was prohibited from publishing during the initial postwar years, he diligently worked on a gigantic futuristic novel of over five hundred pages that later appeared under the title of *Heliopolis*. It was in many regards reminiscent of his earlier opus, *Auf den Marmorklippen*, insofar as it similarly portrayed a struggle between anarchy and order within a framework of fantasy or science fiction. The evident difference was that Jünger now sought to incorporate into the convoluted plot his experiences as an officer and lover in occupied Paris during the war. It is possible to detect autobiographical elements in two of the novel's characters. One is the Regent, who chooses to withdraw from the dispute between two warring factions and, without intervening, to maintain his own sense of moral virtue. He thereby nobly rejects any form of power contradicting his concept of personal freedom. As one commentator has appropriately asked: "Who does not feel thereby reminded of Jünger's behavior in Paris?"[24] A second alter ego is a heroic person named Lucius de Geer, who falls in love with the beautiful and alluring Budur Peri, arguably a veiled personification of Sophie Ravoux, in an affair that ends with the pair escaping on a spaceship to an extraterrestrial exile under the benevolent rule of the Regent (not precisely true to life). If the melodrama of *Heliopolis* was not Jünger's finest hour as a writer, it at least served to portray in fractured form the intense emotions that he had felt during his two long sojourns in Paris.[25]

After the war Jünger returned to Paris for the first time in May 1950, and again several times thereafter. Although he left no extensive record of these visits, it is certain that he retraced his former steps and renewed his old acquaintances there, including Sophie, with whom he had in the meanwhile corresponded. The renewal of their liaison (whether sexual is unclear) could not be hidden from Jünger's wife, conjuring a second major crisis in their marriage. Indeed, Gretha went so far as to write a letter (addressed to Sophie!) indicating her desire for a divorce. She never sent it. But she did confide her anguish to Carl Schmitt, resulting in a confrontation between him and his old friend Jünger that was never resolved. Such intimate details are of course difficult to untangle, but it seems plausible to suppose that they helped to explain his growing estrangement from Paris: "The city gets increasingly on my nerves—I absorbed it quite thoroughly ten years ago, and it cannot add anything new." It followed that he reconciled with Gretha (who later died after a long illness in 1960 at the age of 54), and he began to undertake frequent voyages to more exotic places, everywhere from Sardinia and Egypt to Sumatra and Ceylon.[26]

In December 1948 the Jüngers moved from the British to the French zone of occupation in southwestern Germany. They first lived in Ravensburg, only an hour by car from his brother's home on Lake Constance, and then took up residence near Sigmaringen in the village of Wilflingen at a castle that ironically belonged to Freiherr Franz Schenk von Stauffenberg, a close relative of the man executed—as Jünger was not—for his part in the attempt to assassinate Adolf Hitler in 1944. Now under the more permissive tutelage of France, Jünger was able to resume publication of his writings in conjunction with the Klett-Cotta Verlag in Stuttgart. The eventual outcome was a set of twenty-two volumes of Jünger's collected works. These of course include a new edition of *Strahlungen*, which contained his Paris journals.[27] They are and will forever remain the principal source for any biographical treatment of Ernst Jünger as a German officer, cultural attaché, perceptive witness, dandy, and worldly connoisseur of women and wine in Nazi Paris.

Chapter 10

The Correspondent

Ernst Jünger enjoyed an extraordinarily long life that spanned a period from the last years of the nineteenth century to the threshold of the twenty-first. During all that time he remained remarkably intact, a small and slender person, always immaculately groomed and well dressed whether in uniform or out, compact, with an aquiline nose and steely blue eyes. He was a gentleman, a grand seigneur, the perfect representative of a new European aristocracy of merit. If he was not to the manor born, he remained firmly ensconced in an upper class of intellectual superiority. He moved confidently and elegantly through the high society of those who inhabit a world of good taste. Thus, during the years of the Occupation of Paris, Jünger was a star among stars in the city of cities.

After the end of the Second World War and the beginning of the Cold War, Jünger still had more than half a century to observe and record the doings about him. Yet he did not continue to keep the kind of journals that had encompassed the war years. Instead, he took up with seriousness and great regularity another form of testimony that served many of the same purposes and involved many of the same skills. His postwar correspondence was prodigious, both extensive and voluminous. He composed literally thousands of carefully manicured letters that were exchanged with hundreds of relatives, friends, and fans, nearly all of them of course Europeans. Together, letters written and received, this elaborately archived trove of literary production (for that is what is it was) constituted a remarkable kaleidoscope of Jünger's impressions and reflections across the five decades of his life in the second half of the twentieth century. This massive collection of his correspondence is now housed and catalogued in the German Literature Archive, and it seems inevitable that some enterprising scholar will eventually undertake a systematic analysis of its contents in order to draw a complete portrait of Jünger as an old man, laboring mightily year after year to produce and retain these epistolary remains of the day.

Here, within the confines of a concluding chapter, our objective must necessarily be more modest. Appropriately, the purpose at hand is to select those elements of Jünger's vast *Briefwechsel* that may add a further dimension to our understanding of his career as a German army officer in Paris during the Occupation. Simple logic dictates that this selected correspondence from the war years and thereafter be divided into two categories: German colleagues and French acquaintances. One by one, these personalities may be examined insofar—and no farther—as the extant evidence allows.

Ernst Jünger's contacts in Paris with his fellow officers and German civilian officials mostly occurred in clusters at three locations: while on duty in the Hotel Majestic, at occasional evening gatherings in the nearby Hotel George V (the so-called *Georgsrunde*), or when visiting the regular Thursday salon of Florence Gould. Although these three venues differed somewhat in character, there was of course an overlap among them. For his part, Jünger was a conspicuous figure at all three and was considered a vital member of each. Also, in addition to the regulars of the German administration in Paris, there were sporadic visitations to the French capital by celebrities, notably Martin Heidegger and Carl Schmitt, who could not fail to attract Jünger's attention.

As for military headquarters in the Majestic, virtually no trace remains of the two most senior officers of the MBF, Otto and Heinrich von Stülpnagel. The former left that post in emotional disarray in 1942, then committed suicide in prison right after the war. He apparently had no further contact with Jünger during that time and left no record of it. He was frequently mentioned, however, in other correspondence and memoirs, usually as a rather pathetic individual: "short of stature, with a tendency to posturing and theatrics ... humorless, stiff ... like a tin soldier."[1] Jünger's own later evaluation was distinctly more generous toward Otto's attempts to deter or at least delay what he saw as senseless orders from Berlin (to execute French hostages), which led to his "dismissal"—a word Jünger substituted in a 1952 letter for "resignation," crossed out. Since Heinrich von Stülpnagel's file was destroyed by Jünger for fear of its discovery by the Gestapo, nothing of consequence remains. But Heinrich was universally acclaimed in Jünger's circle of friends as a heroic, noble, and tragic individual, a judgment with which he totally concurred.[2]

A host of more minor characters passed through the corridors of the Majestic, several of whom maintained contact with Jünger after the war: Ernst Schaer, Constantin Cramer von Laue, the director of the German Institute Karl Epting, and also Martin von Katte, who with his wife became a frequent visitor in the Jünger household. Likewise of note was Walter Bargatzky, to whom Jünger confided in 1983 that the Paris years had doubtless left a deep mark on both of them and on all who had served in the Majestic; whenever visiting Paris, Jünger wrote, he always stopped by to stare at the building, "and I stray as in a dream through the corridors, without finding an exit." Yet in his memoirs, published four years later, Bargatzky confessed that he had hardly known Jünger at the time and had read very few of his writings after the war.[3]

Without question, the star of the Majestic crowd and also the fellowship at the George V, where he resided, was Hans Speidel. Clearly it was he who became and remained Jünger's closest friend among members of the senior military administration. Speidel, with an assist from Werner Best, had been responsible for calling Jünger to his post in Paris, where they then collaborated professionally and socialized personally. When Speidel was transferred in April 1942 to the Russian front as chief of staff in the German 8th army, the two corresponded regularly, and they continued to do so in postwar years on a first-name basis with salutations like "*Mein lieber,*" "*stets Dein getreuer,*" etc. It was a sufficient indication of their closeness when, during a visit to Paris in 1952, Speidel took the time to mail to Jünger a menu from his favorite restaurant, the Brasserie Lorraine in the Place des Ternes. Accordingly, Speidel did not neglect to pay tribute to Jünger in his memoir of the war years, published after his retirement from a NATO command in 1977.[4]

Of the other names particularly associated with evenings at the Hotel George V, two are worth mentioning. Horst Grüninger was an enthusiastic fan whose adulation was scarcely reciprocated. Assigned to an artillery school in late 1941, he wrote to Jünger that he was reading constantly from his works and found them to be "magic." Then, stationed in the Soviet Union in 1942, he wrote back repeatedly to Jünger with fond memories of "our island" (meaning the *Georgsrunde*) and "the wonders of Paris." At war's end he worried about "our friend Speidel," reportedly arrested, and complained that he had not heard from Jünger for a long while. There is no record of a response, if any.[5] Altogether different was Jünger's relationship with Clemens Podewils (also known variously in the correspondence as Clemens Graf Podewils, Dr. Podewils, and Clemens Graf von Podewils-Junker-Bigatto), who became acquainted with Jünger in 1941 on a formal basis that later evolved into first names and familiar forms of address. Podewils was often present at the George V and credited Jünger with contributing "a special rhythm" to the soirées there, so that "from an occasional social group emerged a circle." The two stayed in touch, meeting again soon after the war in Kirchhorst and Munich. Their families became closely attached in a harmony that lasted in countless letters until Podewils's death in 1978 at the age of seventy-two. It should be added that friendship does not guarantee a scintillating correspondence, which in this case was filled largely with pleasant commonplaces.[6]

The salon of Florence Gould was intended to promote contacts between German and French intellectuals, and it provided Ernst Jünger with most of his access to Parisian celebrities (of which more below). It followed that the Germans in attendance had to be reasonably proficient in French, for which Jünger certainly qualified. Notable among the others was Gerhard Heller, who held forth at the German Institute and in effect directed it during a long absence of Karl Epting. Heller performed two tasks for Jünger: he provided a contact with Sophie Ravoux during Jünger's stint in Russia, and he passed on information about the weekly sessions chez Florence Gould. She was "an astonishing woman," he wrote to Jünger, especially when she had not imbibed too much champagne.[7] Heller left Paris with the rest of the German administration in August 1944, but he returned frequently after the war and consequently functioned as one of Jünger's contacts with Marcel Jouhandeau, Paul Léautaud, Alfred Fabre-Luce, and Jean Paulhan, as well as Florence Gould herself. In his later memoir, first published in French as *Un Allemand à Paris,* he left a rather gushing account about "the presence of Jünger," who had become "a sort of spiritual father" to him. Although Jünger was "a convinced nationalist," he became increasingly opposed to Hitler and to Nazism, Heller judged, and therefore he favored the resistance movement in Paris, "in which he participated in his fashion." On the basis of this dubious claim, Heller ended by asserting that Jünger thereby offered "a lesson of lucidity and courage." From this laudation one may easily gather that their correspondence was always cordial and often contained mutual reminiscences about "the Valentiner penthouse, the Tour d'Argent, and many other places."[8]

Only slightly less significant for Jünger was perhaps Gerhard Nebel, a frank and devoted admirer who had begun corresponding with the renowned author before the war. Most of Nebel's early letters concerned his attempts to arrange a meeting with Jünger, and apparently Jünger did have some hand in Nebel's transfer to Paris as a translator in September 1941. There enchanted by the air, the women, and the wine, so Nebel wrote, he quickly fell in with the Florence Gould crowd.[9] Later assigned to a tour of duty in Italy, he resumed an exchange of letters with Jünger after the war once he learned that the master had not in fact been murdered, as he had been led to believe. He went on to compose the first primitive biography of Jünger—actually half memoir and half lilting hagiography—in which he enthused that with Jünger's wartime essay *Der Arbeiter* "German prose had reached a tall peak. ... He is a sculptor of language." Probably more defensible was Nebel's perception that Jünger's views on the heroic virtues of war had evolved over time, since he now "sees the soldier almost exclusively in the category of suffering. The warrior is for him no longer the killing and triumphant [conqueror] but one subjected to discipline, threatened by death, exposed to pain."[10] Jünger's subsequent letters to Nebel, whom he had good reason to trust, gave hints of two of his own most basic character traits.

One was Jünger's inveterate nationalism. In 1949 he concluded that his longstanding sympathy for the French was justified: "By comparison, the English remain a spiritless nation"; however, "if one wishes to find spirit (*Geist*) and force united, the German in his best protagonists is still the one who must be sought." Less awkwardly formulated was a second notion of his urge to ethical independence: "All formation of cliques, all spiritual incest is repugnant to me. Everyone should do whatever he considers to be right."[11] That was written in 1949. Nearly two decades later he expressed a similar self-evaluation to Nebel: "I have always conducted myself as a *Freiherr*, [having] little to do as a warrior with soldiers, as a collector [of insects] with entomologists, [or] as an author with contemporary literature." Invariably, in short, he remained a loner.[12]

Another Paris colleague deserves to be added to this list, although he is difficult to locate in the constellation of Jünger's acquaintances. Josef (alias Joseph) Breitbach lived in Paris before, during, and after the war. As a bookman and sometime editor, he knew the city well and had ready access to literary circles there. It was he who had in 1938 introduced the neophyte Jünger to Jean Schlumberger, Julien Green, and André Gide.[13] Files in the Marbach literature archive contain thirty-nine prewar letters from Breitbach to Jünger but, inexplicably, none dated between February 1940 and October 1951. When their correspondence resumed, it was on a sour note. Breitbach made remonstrance about the "bitter tone" in Jünger's comments about a French editor, which reminded him of "unjust complaints" against Jean Schlumberger that Jünger had once made and recently repeated. When Jünger attempted to deflect Breitbach's criticism, the latter replied with a seven-page typed epistle in which he expressed his "deep dismay" with Jünger's unwillingness to detract his wrongheaded opinions. "I am worried about you," he added.[14] Despite this inauspicious confrontation, they soon agreed to leave all unpleasantness aside and to move on (filling three large archival folders with their later correspondence). As often, Jünger's letters were uniformly typed on long sheets of paper, thus eminently suitable as a permanent record of his continuing interest in French intellectual life.

Before turning to that topic, it is worthwhile to take note, as mentioned, of two German celebrities—both occasional visitors to Paris during the Occupation—with whom Jünger had long albeit irregular postwar exchanges. The first was Martin Heidegger. Surely the most prominent of German philosophers of the time, Heidegger was arguably more interested in Jünger's writings than vice versa. This may simply have been because Heidegger could perfectly understand Jünger's prose, whereas Jünger was decidedly out of his metaphysical depth when presented with Heidegger's remarks, as in a 1956 letter informing him about "the transition from not-yet to no-longer" and told that "these two 'not-beingnesses' are not nothing" (*diese beiden "Nicht-seienden" sind nicht nichts*). We can well imagine Jünger's eyes glazing over, as they also must have while perusing the Greek expressions that Heidegger had carefully entered by hand into the typed text of his letter. Obviously he did not know of Jünger's deficient early classical schooling, which had left him with no Greek.[15] Correspond they nonetheless did, at times cordially so, with greetings on special occasions and also from spouse to spouse. Particularly poignant was Heidegger's condolence in 1960 upon learning of the death of Jünger's first wife: "My thoughts are often with you."[16] Yet their expression of shared concerns was always couched in a high degree of verbal formality, which loosened up only very slightly over the years. From the early salutation "*Sehr geehrter Herr Professor,*" Jünger moved cautiously to "*Lieber Herr Heidegger*" and then in 1969, after more than twenty years, to "*Lieber verehrter Martin Heidegger.*" For once, at least as a philosopher, Jünger knew that his place was not at the head of the line.[17]

Martin Heidegger knew it, too. His extended and quite sensible commentaries on Jünger's works have recently been collected into the final (ninetieth!) volume of Heidegger's *Gesamtausgabe,* completed in 2004. Here Jünger is seen as an outstanding disciple of Friedrich Nietzsche—one, however, who fails as a philosopher to transcend his mentor. At least his appreciation of Nietzschean metaphysics exceeded "the very superficial treatment" of it by Oswald Spengler, Heidegger states. It is obvious that Jünger's "writing, thinking, and speaking have been determined by the First World War," a fact that helps to explain his capacity "as no other" to combine the physical with the metaphysical.[18] Yet his limitations are equally evident. "Jünger is an observer (*Erkenner*) but never a thinker." Whereas Nietzsche was a questioner, therefore, Jünger is merely a describer—although, to his credit, he is the "coldest and sharpest" among them. All in all, Heidegger concludes grandly, "Ernst Jünger's entire work is a unique and genuine stance within the basic parameters of Nietzsche, the last metaphysician."[19] Even when compressed here into a brief summary, Heidegger's uncharacteristically simple and uncluttered estimate of Jünger shows that the philosopher well comprehended the virtues and faults of his friend's accomplishments.

The other noteworthy German intellectual celebrity in Jünger's vicinity was the eminent legal theorist Carl Schmitt. Their relationship dated back to 1930, when they were introduced by a faculty member at the University of Leipzig, Hugo Fischer. The two hit it off at once and developed a lasting though problematic friendship, about which Jünger was at least twice warned in no uncertain terms by other correspondents. In 1933, barely three months after the Nazi seizure of power, Fischer wrote that he had given up on Schmitt, who seemed not to realize that "catastrophes" were likely to ensue from a regime that "generally suits the German character." Consequently, a change of course could probably not be expected from within and the nation was thus cursed with its current rulers and their exclusionary policies: "Anyone who doesn't belong to them is an enemy of the people, a pariah."[20] In a 1939 letter to Jünger,

Gerhard Nebel was no less categorical about Schmitt: "I do not like him. He is too much the whore of the current political power, and without any bad conscience, any scruples. ... I hope you are not closely connected with him."[21]

But Jünger was. Despite Schmitt's embrace of the Nazi Party and his apologetics for its sway, Jünger's affection for him was undiminished throughout the war years and beyond. Their letters recounted the former's several visits to Paris, evenings spent with Jünger at the Hotel Ritz, their sharing bottles of wine, and Schmitt's appearances as a lecturer at the German Institute, to which of course Jünger was formally invited. They also had an important personal contact through Schmitt's student Constantin Cramer von Laue, who, we recall, returned to Paris and on crutches encountered Jünger after being severely wounded in action. In the postwar period Jünger more than once took the time to report to Schmitt about his excursions to Paris, where he met with "acquaintances old and new" of mutual interest, including the French philosopher Gabriel Marcel.[22]

Although the archival record is frustratingly incomplete and its visible lacunae sometimes yawning, Ernst Jünger's private correspondence is more than adequate proof of the deep impression that the early 1940s left on his imagination. The German military officers, administrative officials, and assorted intellectuals whom he encountered at that time, and with whom in many instances he maintained direct or indirect contact long thereafter, constituted for Jünger an exclusive fellowship of those who had shared the privilege of serving in Paris during the war years. It must be kept in mind that creating an enduring record of this large and amorphous group of acquaintances was precisely Jünger's intention. The painstaking effort of typing, correcting, filing, and cataloging his correspondence was not casual or incidental for him. It was an essential activity that effectively replaced the earlier keeping of journals. As before, he habitually wrote to be read, whether in the form of a printed volume or an archival manuscript. The critical judgment of scholars, those who might later write an appreciation of him, mattered immensely to Jünger. That being the case, it appears altogether probable that the extant collection of his letters, and the replies to them, was carefully culled so as to remove any document that might reflect badly on him to posterity. Naturally such a hypothesis cannot be proved, but we are obliged to treat this treasure of historical records with the utmost caution.[23]

Any examination of Jünger's correspondence with French intellectuals is bound to be somewhat disappointing. First and above all, it was a great disappointment to Jünger himself. He had hoped to keep abreast of his French friends of the Paris years, but as he sadly confided to Marcel Jouhandeau in 1951, "I probably overestimated their affection for me."[24] Likewise, he admitted to Julien Gracq a year later that "you are correct that many of my erstwhile acquaintances have become silent."[25] One must recall that when Jünger left Paris in August 1944, the city had been under firm military control for more than four years. Suddenly that atmosphere changed, and a time began when it was far less comfortable and potentially quite dangerous for French collaborators to be in any way associated with things German. Jünger did not experience the change, and he displayed little comprehension of the delicate circumstances faced in the immediate postwar period by those he had frequented before his departure. Hence he developed a tendency to exaggerate his personal rejection by all but a handful of Paris correspondents.

With some of them he had in any event established only superficial relationships, and they did not outlast the war. Four prominent names may be placed into that category. In 1942 Henry de Montherlant read the French translation of "Gärten und Strassen" (titled "Routes et Jardins," because the inversion of nouns was phonetically more pleasing), and he thereupon sent a brief note of congratulations to Jünger. Montherlant was struck by the fact that he had passed through many of the same locations during the campaign of 1940, only on the other side of the front, in retreat. He judged from the quality of the author's reactions that Jünger was an "*honnête homme.*"[26] A couple of further messages later that year did not lead to a real connection, and the two probably lost track of each other during Jünger's stay in Russia. Two notorious collaborationists, Jacques Benoist-Méchin and Pierre Drieu la Rochelle, may be mentioned in the same breath. In October 1941 the former, as an official in the Vichy government, sent Jünger a requested list of publications concerning the military events of 1940, as well as a copy of a heretofore censored war journal by Jean Labusquière; nothing ensued.[27] Drieu wrote to Jünger in early 1942 to seek an interview about the Gallimard publishing firm with which both had personal connections. Sent a *laisser passer* for the Hotel Majestic, Drieu forgot to bring it along to the Avenue Kléber and was turned back at the door, after which he also neglected to appear at a dinner party arranged for him and Jünger by Alfred Fabre-Luce. Profuse apologies—"and yet you are one of the rare men in European literature I would like to know better"—were to no avail, and the affair fizzled.[28] The same was true, apparently for another reason, of Jean Cocteau. After meeting Jünger at a social gathering late in 1941, Cocteau wrote three notes in rapid succession to "*mon cher Ernst Jünger,*" in which he displayed more than a casual interest, praising Jünger's flair, his *belle âme*, and his "face so hard and so tender" (*visage si dur et si doux*). Coming from France's most famous homosexual, these words were at the least ambiguous, especially with Cocteau's assurances that he and Jünger in fact shared the same country "light and high where the heart is at ease." He closed with a plea that they meet again soon ("*Voyons nous vite*"). From these shards of evidence we may gather that Cocteau was manifestly attracted by Jünger's celebrity status and sleek appearance. But, if so, the presumption must be that any ambitions by Cocteau to launch a courtship were thwarted by Jünger's evident heterosexuality.[29]

A second category of French intellectuals comprised those whom Jünger encountered before or during the Occupation and with whom he had some correspondence afterward. These included, for instance, Jean Schlumberger, Julien Gracq, Abel Bonnard, and Paul Léautaud. Of these, only the last made a noteworthy impression on Jünger, who later translated one of Léautaud's writings into German, an essay entitled "In Memoriam," in sad remembrance of his departed father. However, this task may have been undertaken by Jünger less as a testimony to Léautaud's literary brilliance than as a tribute to his own late and repeatedly lamented father.[30]

Two of Jünger's other correspondents stood at opposite ends of the political spectrum. Louis-Ferdinand Céline was ferociously pro-fascist during the Occupation, creating for Jünger "the impression of a maniac who cannot really be made responsible for his declarations." In 1951 the appearance of a French translation of Jünger's *Pariser Tagebücher* contained a most unflattering portrait of "Merlin," identifiably Céline, causing the latter to threaten legal action for defamation. This imbroglio dragged on for months despite Jünger's apologies to Céline—"I do not approve of your views, but nothing lies farther from me than to harm you"—and his willingness to deny any intended reference to him.[31] Quite a different reason explained the limitation of Jünger's contacts with Jean Paulhan, whom he had met in Paris along with Léautaud and others at the Thursday salon of Florence Gould. Evidently unaware of Paulhan's close connections with the French Resistance, Jünger maintained cordial though never close relations with him during the Occupation and, through Gerhard Heller, into the late 1940s. Then, in 1951, their mutual interest was briefly rekindled when Paulhan wrote to Jünger requesting the contribution of an essay on André Gide for a special edition of the (already defunct) *Nouvelle Revue Française*. Jünger complied and was rewarded with a charming note of thanks from Paulhan plus the gift of a book. Yet the Marbach archive contains no further evidence of direct contacts between the two.[32]

One other name in this category deserves comment. Perhaps because he detected in Jünger a somewhat ambiguous attitude toward the Occupation, much like his own, Alfred Fabre-Luce wished to publish an excerpt of Jünger's writings in an anthology planned by the publisher Plon and invited him to join in discussions of it. Furthermore, Fabre-Luce found lofty praise for the German's skill in portraying the eternal amid the temporal. He wrote in 1942 that the discovery of this work—presumably meaning the French version of *In Stahlgwittern*—was "among the most important events of my year. Your sense of style and your gifts as a moralist are well suited to seduce a French reader."[33] After the war Fabre-Luce's salutations to Jünger graduated from "*cher monsieur*" to "*cher ami*," even though they rarely if ever met and maintained personal contact mostly though their mutual friend Hans Speidel. In addition, Fabre-Luce had a very particular motive. He had in the early 1950s published his *Histoire de la Révolution Européenne,* the central thesis of which was that France and Germany were destined to share a common future, no strange notion for Jünger. But whereas the book was thought by some circles in Paris to be unduly pro-German, Fabre-Luce complained, it was refused for translation by the Piper Verlag in Munich for being too anti-German. Did Jünger know another more willing publisher in Germany? Apparently not. Months passed without a contract and without Jünger's continuing interest. The exchange of pleasant communications by mail nonetheless continued into the 1960s.[34]

One name remains in a category of its own for closeness and cordiality, that of Marcel Jouhandeau. Starting during the Occupation with *"cher ami"* and extending until his death in 1979, no other French personality enjoyed remotely the same degree of familiarity with Ernst Jünger as did Jouhandeau. Before August 1944 the two were often seen strolling together, sometimes arm in arm, or chatting behind a bottle of wine in a sidewalk café.[35] Although a lapse of direct contact for several years occurred right after the war, they were remembered to one another repeatedly by Gerhard Heller, then resident in Paris. Writing in German, Jünger resumed correspondence with Jouhandeau in 1951, observing that he was now the one occupied and regretting that he had lost touch with most of his former acquaintances in Paris. He also took up the controversy with Céline, attributing it to an "error" by his French editor of which he had no knowledge. Jünger was obviously worried about his fading reputation in France and wondered if Jouhandeau could help to rescue it. Jouhandeau's reply conveyed his delight with the note, although "I was not able to understand the entire message," which he had passed on to Jean Paulhan for explanation. In any case, he assured Jünger, certain persons did not need to be near in order to be present.[36]

In mutual admiration, Jünger praised Jouhandeau as one who did not hesitate to defend those no longer in vogue, a trait that distinguished him from most of his Paris colleagues. "That is why," Jünger wrote just before a visit to the French capital in 1958, "you are about the only one among them that I am going to see." This letter was signed with *"tout mon coeur."*[37] There is no need to pursue this exercise in amiability any further, except to underscore an article, "In Recognition of Ernst Jünger," published by Jouhandeau in 1965 in the literary journal *Antaios.* In it he recalled Jünger's debut at the Florence Gould salon in the Hotel Bristol, where he made a modest entrance in civilian garb, far from what the French expected from a German war hero. One of those most impressed, he remembered, was Jean Cocteau, who referred to Jünger as "a silver fox." It may have seemed strange to some Parisians that Jouhandeau formed such a close relationship with a German officer during the Occupation, Jouhandeau wrote, but few Germans had ever developed as refined a taste for things French or such a passionate attachment to Paris. Besides, he added, "our relationship had *je ne sais quoi* of timelessness."[38] Little wonder, then, that in later correspondence Jouhandeau's "*Ernst très cher*" was reciprocated by Jünger's "*bien à toi.*" These salutations provided a fitting conclusion to a friendship and a correspondence over many decades that can only be described as most affectionate.[39]

It bears repeating that the foregoing survey of Jünger's correspondence, specifically letters from and to him concerning Paris, cannot possibly aspire to be definitive, simply because the extant evidence cannot warrant such a claim. Nevertheless, as a whole, it adds an indispensable dimension to Jünger's wartime experience in France, which continued to preoccupy him throughout the rest of his life. All things considered, Marcel Jouhandeau's words of praise for Jünger do not appear to be inappropriate as an epitaph. If he often remained aloof or indifferent to persons, causes, or tragedies, his attraction to France was genuine and lasting.

(DLA – Marbach)

Jünger in a postwar photo dedicated to Banine, whose married name is deleted

(author's photo)
Jünger's favorite sidewalk restaurant at the Place des Ternes

(author's photo)
Tombstone of Sophie and Paul Ravoux in the cemetery of Montparnasse

(author's photo)

Sophie Ravoux's apartment building at 72 Rue du Cherche-Midi

Sophie Ravoux as a young woman during the Occupation

(DLA – Marbach)

(DLA – Marbach)

Sophie Ravoux in later life

Postscript

LIEBE SOPHIE

It would be a genuine service to scholarship if the archives of Ernst Jünger's correspondence were edited for publication, especially his exchange with Sophie Ravoux. That day has not yet come. Pending this eventuality, the historian can at least serve to summarize as succinctly as possible the contents of these documents and to quote enough of them to convey their distinct flavor. These letters tell a story—the inside story of Jünger's affective life—that cannot be found elsewhere. Anyone, however, who approaches them with the expectation of making a sensational discovery is likely to be disappointed. The record is incomplete and often inconclusive. Yet it allows us to unravel certain personal relationships that are thereby convincingly, if only partially, revealed. Caution and discretion are in order, of course, since any such analysis must remain both subjective and speculative.

These generalities apply in particular to the years of the German Occupation in Paris while Jünger was stationed there. Not counting his occasional flirtations with French women during the early days after 10 May 1940, three of his female acquaintances stand out. They may be distinguished here, to be direct, according to levels of intimacy: one with whom he apparently had no physical relationship, one with whom he possibly might have had, and one with whom he certainly did have.

Banine: Umm-El-Banine Assadoulaeff was a strange and somewhat exotic creature. Born into a Muslim family in the Caucasus near Baku, where her wealthy father was an oil magnate, she was raised speaking Russian and, thanks to a Baltic governess, German. Married against her will at fifteen, she left her home and husband two years later, boarding the Orient Express in Constantinople, bound for France. There she became utterly French and found an architect from Toulouse with whom she experienced a second unhappy marriage. Separated and single, she lived in a small flat in the Rue Lauriston, parallel to the Avenue Kléber, five minutes from the Hotel Majestic. One day in October 1942, gathering her courage, she wrote a note to "*cher maître*" Ernst Jünger, as she simply explained, because "you are one of the two authors that I currently admire the most." She had read *Auf den Marmorklippen* in French translation, "literally a magic book," and she hoped to meet the author, "an immense talent." To these flattering approaches Jünger scratched a brief reply in German, explaining that he was just leaving for the Eastern front. In turn, Banine expressed her "great joy" at the prompt reply and a hope to see her hero when he returned to Paris.[1]

Jünger's reappearance in early 1943 soon led to notes, phone calls, and a visit to Banine's apartment. Thereafter they met from time to time, but the end of the Occupation resulted in a rupture of nearly two years, during which time she divested herself of both her maiden and married names, preferring to be called by her plain *nom de plume*, Banine. In 1946 she translated, without Jünger's input, his essay "Der Friede," which appeared in France as "La Paix." In appreciation, Jünger wrote a letter from Kirchhorst, addressing her as "*Liebe Madame Banine*," adding "I think often of you" and signing with his personal monogram (which appeared later on the cover of his books). Despite a mutual hesitancy, which slowly dissipated, to adopt more familiar terms of address, they became steady pen pals.[2]

During the early postwar years Banine performed an important function for Jünger by providing an easy conduit to Sophie Ravoux, with whom she became closely acquainted in Paris. At first referring to Sophie as "the lady" or "Madame R.," Banine soon settled on "Gypsy" as an apt nickname for one who had seemingly lost her bearings in life.[3] In September 1946 Sophie visited Banine for the first time in the Rue Lauriston. The latter expected her to be tall, slender, and quiet. Instead, she was the opposite: small, shapely, and lively. They had a three-hour conversation during which Jünger was the sole topic. The two got on well enough, but Banine noticed that Sophie "appears to be bored with her life and absolutely not to know what to do with her days." In general, Jünger did not comment on these frequent reports, and only twice did he pass on greetings to "Gipsy" (*sic*), although he did once add a tempting remark: "In recent days I have again dreamed of her, as I often do."[4]

There was another matter. Besides Sophie's evident lassitude, Banine told Jünger, "she does not seem to be very happy with her husband." Released from captivity at war's end, Paul Ravoux took up journalism again and became a French newspaper correspondent in Bonn and Berlin. Banine met him in Paris and was thoroughly unimpressed: "One cannot imagine anyone more unsympathetic," she wrote. "He displeased me to such a point that I cannot explain it." Indeed, Banine commented on Sophie's marriage as "idiotic, like most marriages"—a line written, to be sure, by a young woman already twice divorced.[5]

In the summer of 1947 Sophie left for three weeks in Berlin, to join her husband, not before relaying through Banine her address and conveying the wish that Jünger write to her there. He did not do so, provoking Sophie's sorrowful regrets, duly reported back to Jünger by Banine. Sophie also spent time in Cannes, but she returned to Paris very discontented—"Alas, she is that very often," Banine rather cattily remarked.[6] By now, the end of 1947, this comment fell into a clearly emerging pattern of Banine's cynicism toward Sophie, and it indicated that their relationship was perceptibly cooling. In December "Gypsy" made no contact with Banine for weeks and suddenly canceled a scheduled meeting, "pretending" that her husband was taking up all her time. "No, in reality she does not want to come to see me," Banine concluded, the reason being that "she supposes that you have spoken to me in a rather confidential manner that leaves no doubt about your relationship [with Sophie]," whereas "she has never been open with me."[7]

Evidently, this tale might have provided excellent fodder for a soap opera. It has been related here in some detail because it provides two essential explanations about Jünger. One was that his correspondence with Banine began to lose much of its relevance for him once the falling out between the two women in Paris choked off a regular and reliable source of information about Sophie. Second, the narrative also confirms that an unsubtle eroticism in Banine's relationship to Jünger was developing apace. Rather than a conduit for Sophie, Banine was becoming her rival, undermining her rapport with Jünger at every turn. In 1950 Banine published a slender volume entitled *Rencontres avec Ernst Jünger* in which she gave a fair account of how they had met and become friends. But she neglected to mention two crucial items: the importance and evolution of her relationship with Sophie Ravoux and a frank admission of her confused sexual hankering for Jünger.[8]

It is unnecessary to reconstruct this part of the story, especially when a few quotations from Banine's letters can make the situation indelibly clear. In July 1950, in response to a previous communication with Jünger (of which there is no record), she asked and answered a question: "Am I still your slave? I fear that I shall remain so all of my life, whatever happens, even if for example another man enters my life, even if I remarry." To this she added: "This slavery is the punishment for my reprehensible conduct with other men." Rapidly the level of intimacy was rising, as when a fortnight later Banine pleaded: "Dear Ernst, tell me things about yourself and your life. I miss you." Then, in September, she addressed him as "my dearest friend."[9] Finally, on 2 October, Banine abandoned all restraint: "I will not ask more of you if you come to Paris this autumn, so as not to discomfort you, but know once and for all that I am forever your slave, ready to greet you even in a chilly apartment, ready to do anything you want, and ready to fulfill all of your fantasies, even the most bizarre." Such a frank proposition surely requires no commentary.[10]

Thereupon, without explanation, a gap of one year in the Jünger–Banine correspondence occurs in the Marbach archive. There is no doubt that some communications continued to flow between them, but they have either been lost or, far more likely, culled from the collection of letters. It is nonetheless all but certain, judging from subsequent notes, that Jünger finally rejected Banine's advances. To verify that assumption one need only fast-forward to the spring of 1952, when Banine bitterly complained to Jünger about the "drama" in her life caused by his refusal to come to Paris in the previous autumn. He had repeatedly avoided every occasion to see her again, she insisted, thus making it obvious "that you did not care about it much or, rather, at all."[11] Furthermore, Jünger had written to her that "you should not harass me" (*Sie dürfen mich nicht plagen*). That was far from her intention, Banine replied: "Besides, in disappearing from his life, I do not see how I could 'harass' a man who has never demonstrated for me other than an indifference scarcely tinged with benevolence." For this cutting and, it would appear, definitive statement about Jünger's restraint in his personal contacts with her, Banine soon apologized and promised not to annoy him anymore with her letters, closing: "Adieu, my dear angel."[12]

If Banine intended at this point to end her relations with Jünger altogether, she failed. They continued to exchange messages for another forty years. Yet the spark was extinguished. There were no more reports on Sophie and no further mention of slavery. In a 1971 *Portrait d'Ernst Jünger*, the somewhat warmed-over and extended version of her earlier account of him, Banine came squarely to terms with Jünger's second marriage, describing Liselotte Jünger as "the ideal spouse." But she also offered a less than truthful record of her own part in working out her personal attachment to Jünger. Her concerns about their close relationship (that is, whether it might contain an erotic component) proved to be frivolous, she explained, since Jünger displayed no undue familiarity but instead a perfectly correct simplicity, "a simplicity encouraged, it is true, by my determination to allow Jünger to live according to his own tastes and not according to mine." Squaring that statement with her actual performance as a seductress is, to say the least, difficult.[13] The two nevertheless maintained a genuine cordiality to the end, and it was altogether justified for the *Figaro* to begin Banine's obituary in October 1992 by announcing "the death of a great friend of Ernst Jünger."[14]

Florence Gould: Born in San Francisco of French parents in 1895 (exactly Ernst Jünger's age), Florence Lacaze grew into adolescence as an American girl and then moved to France with her mother. There she became, except for a very slight accent, an intelligent, athletic, and cultured Parisian woman of high society. That society became ever higher when she married Frank Jay Gould, billionaire son of the railway magnate Jay Gould. During the First World War she served in Limoges as a nurse and then, after her marriage, moved to a grand villa on the Riviera, where, if we believe an article published in the German journal *Madame* in 1990, she took numerous lovers with whom she danced into the wee hours at exclusive nightclubs. According to this source, she told a friend in 1960: "Ah, in our circles during the thirties we had nonstop affairs. Practical, don't you think?" Whether that statement was apocryphal or not, undoubtedly Florence brought an illustrious reputation to her career as a social animal in occupied Paris during the Second World War.[15]

A 1983 essay in *Le Monde* by Dominique Aury described Florence Gould as a "tiny, vivacious, and blonde" woman with "admirable shoulders and pretty legs." She also had strikingly large blue eyes, which she usually preferred to hide behind dark glasses. She possessed the easy affability of many Americans who quickly establish a first-name basis with recent acquaintances. Thus, from every point of view, she was perfectly adapted to preside over the regular Thursday evening soirées that met in Paris after 1941, first in the Hotel Bristol, then at her lavish apartment in the Avenue Malakoff, between the Avenue Foch and the Porte Maillot. There she received the crème of Paris crème, effortlessly mixing French celebrities with resident German intellectuals like Ernst Jünger.[16]

Florence's part in Jünger's life while he was a military officer of the Occupation can be quickly told because the evidence left from it is so sparse. From what is known, it is possible but not certain that they shared, at least briefly, a sexual episode. The grounds for such a suspicion are several. First, there was Florence's previous reputation as a promiscuous femme fatale, something she never denied and which there is little reason to doubt. Second, there is the intriguing repeated use by Jünger of pseudonyms in reference to her, a practice that he adopted in his journals (notably alluding to Sophie Ravoux) in order to hide or diffuse the identity of persons close to him, such as a lover. Whether this was the case of "Lady Orpington," "Armance," or perhaps also "Mme. Scrittore"—alias Florence Gould—is uncertain but not at all improbable.[17] Third, the testimony of Gerhard Heller, a regular guest at those Thursday evening gatherings and a close friend of both, disclosed that Jünger was more than a casual flirt for Florence, "with whom he became intimately connected," though the level of that intimacy was left unspecified.[18] Finally, three suggestive scraps of evidence are extant in the Marbach archive. The first is an undated note, obviously written very formally by Florence Gould soon after Jünger's arrival in Paris in 1941: an invitation to join her salon at the Hotel Bristol on the next Thursday evening at 8 PM. A second card, also undated, was quite different in tone, employing the familiar form of address to "my dear Ernst," wishing him a good trip (probably to Russia in November 1942) and a quick return. This message closed: "I regret not to have embraced you before your departure." Just how literally that common expression was intended remained tantalizingly vague, perhaps even for Jünger. The file also contains the record of a telephone message, relayed through a hotel clerk in September 1943, in which Florence apologized to Jünger for having to cancel their planned promenade that day because of an illness, a confirmation that their contacts were not confined to convivial group gatherings with others.[19]

Manifestly, such bits and pieces do not add up to a certainty, but they do show that Jünger's social life in Paris was humming with possibilities, of which he may have, given the occasion, taken advantage.

Sophie Ravoux: In the Paris cemetery of Montparnasse, Division 13, lies the austere burial site of Sophie Ravoux and her husband, Paul. Besides their names and dates, one other nugget of information is chiseled into the gravestone beneath the bare inscription for Sophie: "*née* Koch." She left no memoir and rarely spoke to others (Banine was an exception) about her relationship with Ernst Jünger, something about which her tomb is also silent. One might never suspect that she was other than the faithful wife of the partner in marriage with whom she rests forever buried. But the recently granted access to Sophie's extensive correspondence with Jünger offers irrefutable proof that he indeed became, during the Occupation of Paris, and that he remained so for fifty years thereafter, the man of her life.

Sophie Koch was born and reared in Magdeburg, Germany, a rather bleak industrial city on the Elbe southwest of Berlin. Little is known of her early life except that she completed her secondary schooling in Magdeburg and began medical studies at the University of Freiburg im Breisgau. In a 1985 letter she recounted how she, like many other students who have spent a winter semester there, had fifty-five years earlier caught the Höllenthalbahn to Hinterzarten for several weekends of skiing. That was about 1930.[20] Within a few years, however, she moved permanently to France, where she completed her education and became a physician. Why the change? The answer may simply be that she visited Paris and fell in love with the city and her future husband. But she may also have been clairvoyant enough to realize that a Jewish family affiliation on her mother's side might pose a serious problem for her in Germany after 1933. In any event, she chose to marry Paul Ravoux and to take up residence with him in a quite handsome sandstone apartment building, still standing, at 72 Rue du Cherche-Midi in the sixth arrondissement of Paris.[21]

As a journalist, Paul Ravoux's outspoken and written anti-fascism could not fail to gain the attention of the Gestapo once France was defeated in 1940 and the German Occupation began. His imprisonment and then incarceration in a concentration camp during the later war years left Sophie, as a straw widow with no children, alone. It was therefore not surprising that her eyes met with Ernst Jünger's one day in 1942 at the Hotel Majestic, where she had come on some official business. They became well acquainted during Jünger's first tour of duty in the French capital, when they began the practice of taking long walks together in various neighborhoods and parks of the city.[22] While Jünger was stationed in the Soviet Union they corresponded frequently, and Sophie did not miss an opportunity to remind him of the "enchantment" of Paris. Both of them regularly composed their letters in German, which must have encouraged a kind of complicity that increasingly led Sophie to express her feelings in an unguarded fashion: should she not see him again soon, she wrote in December 1942, "do not believe that I therefore think of you less often and intensely than I do today." Simultaneously, she began to reveal to him the troubled state of her marriage. Shortly after Paul Ravoux's arrest, she admitted that "my personal life has now become so difficult that I ask myself with concern how it will be later. It has become almost impossible, mutually.... Now it is very difficult."[23] Meanwhile, after his assignment in Russia, Jünger's long furlough in Kirchhorst with his wife Gretha was not mentioned to Sophie, to whom Claus Valentiner made excuses for his friend's delayed arrival back in Paris.[24] Understandably, Jünger's second tour in the Paris Occupation, at a time in which he and Sophie saw each other nearly every day, left no cache of letters between them. All that remains is a note of mid-August 1944, typed in French by Sophie while enclosing a pressed flower, in which she deplored that "*Cher Monsieur Jünger*" had departed "too soon." It was signed with best wishes and fond memories by one of Sophie's favorite pseudonyms, "Mme. Armenoville."[25]

Unmistakably, Sophie's letters after the German withdrawal from Paris had a rather pathetic quality. Jünger had written on his way back to Germany to inform her of the death of his son Ernstel. She replied in August 1945 with sympathetic *billets doux*: "I have thought of you so often" and "My thoughts have often been with you. Again and again I think back to our walks and conversations.... I have been very worried about you." As for herself, Sophie was consumed by self-pity: "Never have I been so destitute, helpless, alone, and unhappy." She signed off with "*toujours.*" Five weeks later she wrote again, complaining that she had not heard from him since April: "Who knows whether the faint voices of the past still reach you, since the call of the present is perhaps too *strong*. Who knows whether you still think, as often I do, about our beautiful strolls. Maybe you have already forgotten *la bonne Sophie*?" Finally, pleading: "How are you? Do not entirely forget me."[26]

Ernst Jünger had not forgotten Sophie Ravoux, but it can safely be assumed that his thoughts were now mixed with a sense of estrangement. His first long letter to her was not written until January 1946, nearly sixteen months after his flight from Paris. He described his move to St.-Dié in Lorraine, the return to Germany, his brief command of a *Volkssturm* unit, and then the tragic news of his elder son's death "that struck especially my wife so hard that I am still today worried about her." It was his only reference to Gretha. He recalled mutual friends in Paris—Heller, Valentiner, and others—but also, as a bow to Sophie, he mentioned their walks around the city "that were marked by strict tradition," a remark that reflected how Jünger never let his guard down in public and had probably not held hands with her, let alone hugging or kissing in the street. This rather cool sentiment was followed by an enigmatic closing: "So it was, so it is, so it shall be." But what was "it"?[27]

This letter, apparently the last that Ernst Jünger would write to "*Liebe Sophie*" for almost twenty years, proved to be the raising of the guillotine. We may be sure that at some point in time between the beginning of 1946 and September 1948, Jünger found it necessary to inform her—possibly with a note or more probably by telephone—that their relationship would have to end. The agonizing response from Paris was dated only 3 March, "Wednesday, after a painful promenade." The year was doubtless 1948. With no news recently from him, Sophie had become alarmed that he was not well, but then came the awful truth: "Now I am in sorrow. I am losing you." Writing in French, unlike her previous letters, she poured out her heart: "I don't know if you realize what the year you gave me meant to me and how happy I was. I know that now better than in the past. A year full of incomparable happiness." The time since his departure from France had been unbearable: "I allowed myself to go on feeling loved. Life and days without you lacked color. I missed you and I did not live. I existed." Sophie claimed to have neither regret nor resentment about Jünger's leaving. "But I am very unhappy. I would have wanted to surround you with more tenderness, more appreciation, than I showed in the past." Then she came to the heart of the matter: 'I am now alone. I want everything to be restored [with Gretha in Kirchhorst] as you desire. It causes me great pain to say that because I am losing you. Yet I anticipated and dreaded this moment, and I knew I would suffer, but I did not expect it so soon. For the one who loves, it is always too soon." Clearly Sophie did have both regret and resentment. She had discovered another Ernst Jünger: "The heart closed. With harsh words, as if the facts were not already enough. At that moment I had a dreadful pain." No doubt he, too, had known unhappiness, but his was temporary and curable. Hers was not. "What pain for me not to see you anymore, nor to hear you, nor to feel, nor to wait for you, nor to live with you and walk at your side." In the end she could only give thanks "for all-all-all." Still, she continued, "is it not necessary to say *adieu*, that terrible word, cruel and hateful?" In fact, they were after all to exchange hundreds of letters, notes, and cards over the next five decades, but never again would such strong emotion be so agonizingly expressed.[28]

It would have been typical for Jünger to integrate Sophie's epistle into his private archive, and presumably he did so. But in the fall of 1948, for reasons obscure (did he deliberately pull it out?), this document fell into the hands of his spouse Gretha. She thereupon typed a scathing letter to Sophie that began with the abrupt and chilling salutation of "Madame." Heretofore, she wrote, Banine had served as a link between Kirchhorst and Paris, but now the time had come for a direct contact. In 1943, when Gretha first learned of the situation in Paris (meaning her husband's presumed infidelity), she was prepared to grant him a divorce—not from any sympathy for Sophie but because of their difference in attitude: "You attempted to fight, [whereas] I had too much natural pride to seek this sort of arena in which I do not feel comfortable." But Ernst returned home, and he did so voluntarily, as Sophie herself recognized when she wrote of a "curable" sorrow. Here Gretha quoted, albeit not precisely, a passage from Sophie's anguished letter to Jünger—indicating that it might have been somewhat edited before mailing. Gretha then brought a charge that may not appear to be entirely justified: "Although you felt at that time, in your words, that his heart was closed, you tried everything to arrange another meeting, not without reason, since you know his weaknesses as well as I do." Her husband had been fully informed and he was free to go, but Gretha placed one immutable condition for his remaining with her: "the complete termination of all relations with you." That still held. The doors were open, and Gretha would make no attempt to restrain her spouse or to prevent Sophie from contacting him: "You are free to come to Kirchhorst or to meet with him at some suitable place. You will not encounter the slightest obstacle from me." Signed, without salutation, Gretha Jünger.[29]

This biting message was written, as the Germans say, *von oben herab,* from a position of superiority; and it can fairly be classified as a *coup de grâce.* Almost an entire decade ensued before Sophie wrote another letter to Jünger, "after all the long years," in response to a note from him about a possible trip to Paris, where he had visited a few times in the meanwhile without contacting her. She was often absent, spending time with her husband in Berlin or her parents in Baden. From time to time she had sent Jünger greeting cards, but they went unanswered, forcing her to conclude: "Ernst has completely forgotten me, and I will also answer no more." Yet she found the complete separation difficult to bear, she wrote to him, and she especially missed their promenades in Paris. She was likely to be there in the spring and summer. Addressing Jünger now in the familiar form, she added: "I would gladly see you once again. Would you also want to?" As in years past, she signed "*la bonne Sophie.*"[30]

These inviting words were written barely three weeks before the death of Paul Ravoux in 1957. Coincidentally, it was also precisely at a time when Ernst Jünger learned that his wife was suffering from an incurable cancer. The thought that he and Sophie might both soon be widowed must have crossed their minds. Certainly it crossed Sophie's, and in the months that followed she made it clear that she was alone and available: "I have no idea what I will do now. … I am very sad," she wrote in early 1958; and again: "I will need sun and human warmth, since I am now completely alone."[31] Jünger cannot be accused of encouraging her. True, he wrote a note of regret about Paul Ravoux's passing, but he did not communicate again for a year. In the meantime Sophie was back in Paris, and she promptly assured him that she could be reached at the same address and phone number in the Rue du Cherche-Midi. He did visit Paris briefly in the summer of 1960 and saw her there, after which she sent a photo of herself, saying that his presence had awakened slumbering memories and "did me good." She closed "affectionately."[32] It would be inadmissible to make too much of a single salutation, but one cannot overlook the context: a series of messages from her following Gretha Jünger's death in November 1960. Repeatedly Sophie proposed that Jünger meet with her, whenever and wherever, and she reiterated her lament about loneliness: "*Je me sens perdu au monde.*" She scolded that Jünger did not write and professed to worrying that his silence was due to bad health: "I am somewhat anxious." Maybe she could take a train to visit him? Maybe they could spend the holidays in Paris? And so forth.[33]

There is no way to estimate to what extent Sophie's hopes to reestablish close personal ties with Jünger were rising. She was plagued by doubts and self-doubts: "[I] am sometimes rather tired of this existence [and] I am numbed by loneliness." She wondered in February 1962 when they could meet again, adding: "But maybe your desire to do so is not so great."[34] Her intuition was correct. A few days later she received word from Jünger that he was planning to remarry. "Your letter brought me a huge and somewhat unexpected surprise," she answered. Somewhat? Sophie was in shock again, but with a difference. This time she was soon resigned: "I will continue my solitary life. Sometimes I think it is my destiny to be so alone." She closed plaintively: "Don't forget your old Sophie."[35] Thereafter Jünger scarcely ever wrote without mentioning his second wife Liselotte, and Sophie ordinarily sent greetings to her as a postscript to her letters. After the wedding, conspicuously, the Marbach archive contains no message between them for a full year.

Effectively, the story ended there, or it faded away. Dozens of personal messages followed, by mail, by phone, and with increasing frequency by postcard. But the tensions and the longings of earlier days were gone. Everyone behaved with admirable dignity, to the point that Ernst Jünger could visit Paris and even stay in Sophie's flat, while she could reciprocate by traveling to the Jünger residence in Wilflingen to spend a few days with the captain and his wife (they were usually addressed as "*Herr und Frau Hauptmann*" by fellow villagers). Unfortunately Sophie's health began to crumble from arthritis, rheumatism, influenza, and so on, not to dwell on her long episodes of painfully extracted teeth and inserted dentures. She also fell badly in 1972 after tripping over a suitcase in the railway station of Strasbourg, breaking her foot and forcing her to hobble for months with crutches or a cane.[36] Meanwhile, remaining in character, Jünger stood erect and indomitable, ever the "grey fox" that Jean Cocteau had once so much admired. But he, too, was aging, and the signals from his direction grew weaker. There was an occasional flash, as in 1984 when Jünger sent Sophie the copy of a new edition of *Strahlungen* in which "the Doctoresse" frequently appeared. Her search of it aroused "old memories." How could they forget what they had shared? "And," she fittingly commented with simple elegance, "everything is enclosed in a wonderful garden to which no one else holds the key."[37]

Ernst Jünger died in 1998; Sophie Ravoux, in the year 2001.

Conclusion

To say that Ernst Jünger's person, his career, and consequently his writings were filled with ambiguity is to stretch the limits of the obvious. For that reason this study of his tours of duty as a German officer during the Occupation of Paris after 1940, the most significant period of his adulthood, began with the word *Einzelgänger,* and it needs to end there as well.

If such a defining notion is to be taken seriously, however, scholarly estimations of Jünger should by all means avoid historical reductionism. A number of researchers, for example, have attempted to portray him as a proto-fascist or at least a fellow traveler who flirted with Nazism and fundamentally accepted its aggressive and destructive principles. As one biographer has said, Jünger adopted "extreme right-wing positions" that were "reactionary in the extreme," and hence "it can be agreed that Jünger stands about as far to the right as one can imagine."[1] But such a categorical judgment is much too simplistic to capture an intellect as complex as Jünger's. True, he hailed from a conservative bourgeois background from which his erratic formal education and his early traumatic experience in the First World War allowed him little escape. Yet Jünger's inquiring mind, his extraordinarily wide reading, and his broad circle of acquaintances offered him ample opportunities to adopt an increasingly nuanced perspective on political and historical development. His express reservations about Adolf Hitler and the "frumpy" NSDAP cannot be brushed aside, nor his dim view—frequently and clearly stated in his Paris journals—of the Nazi Party's anti-Semitism and plans for a Final Solution. To reduce Jünger to an inveterate and immutable right-winger during the Weimar and Nazi years therefore seems inadmissible as a key to understanding his complicated thoughts and reactions throughout three long decades.

Another evaluation of Jünger departs from the postulate that he represented a particularly German form of European "dandyism" in the early twentieth century. Here the assumption is that everything was fodder for his mill of aestheticism, and surely Jünger supplied some evidence for this conception of his character, witness the often cited episode of strawberries and wine on the roof of the Hotel Raphael. Repeatedly Jünger has been portrayed as a boulevard dandy in Paris, attending exclusive salons and fancy restaurants, oblivious to or at least uncaring about the suffering of others; thus he recognized evil but did little to condemn or oppose it.[2] Certainly there is some truth to these accusations. But again, there is a distinctly reductionist tone to this appreciation of Jünger, which has the disadvantage of containing a conclusion within its initial premise. Like Jünger the reactionary, Jünger the aesthete is trapped in a single category that robs him of complexity and in effect predetermines any consideration of his comportment before, during, and after his stay as military officer and cultural attaché in Paris.

It therefore appears best to characterize Captain Jünger, rather, as a person lacking structured and systematic thinking. This blurred focus was of course partly a result of his uncompleted schooling and his failure to develop any compelling intellectual discipline. Unquestionably, moreover, he had a talent for evasion when it came to sustaining or elaborating some activity at length, a condition perhaps verging on an attention disorder. Yet his dilettantism was at least of high order, as an assembled list of his voracious reading would easily attest. Accordingly, the literary form of the daily journal was perfectly suited to Jünger's temperament, just as his playful sexual proclivities as a young man doubtless expressed a spiritual restlessness. The "Captain's Paradise" of Kirchhorst and Paris, Gretha and Sophie, was well suited for an individual of such talents and inclinations. As for his *Pariser Tagebücher*, Jünger's cultivated way of life obviously involved self-censorship, repeated evasion of responsibility for himself and his friends, occasional fictionalization or transposition of dreams and reality, and always a stylization of his prose.

Finally, it followed that Jünger was consumed by self-contradictions. Several antimonies come readily to mind: military man and cultural envoy, depression and exhilaration, pessimism and optimism, romanticism and realism, and so forth. Above all, although in general he expressed a keen interest in nature and the human condition, he still maintained an aloof distance even from those closest to him. No wonder others sometimes decided that he was not to be counted on. *Désinvolture* was the term he chose to describe himself. We might more simply conclude that he was a troubled—and troubling—loner, one who went his own way.

The Life and Work of Allan Mitchell
1933–2016
Volker Berghahn

Allan Mitchell, the renowned historian of Franco-German relations in the nineteenth and twentieth centuries, passed away on 30 October 2016, after an operation from which he sadly did not recover.*

Allan was among those historians whose contributions to scholarship may have been underestimated during his lifetime, and it is only when we look back on his writings and academic accomplishments that we can see how significant a contribution he has made to modern European History. True, he once called himself an "outsider" to the profession, but this may apply only to his position in the community of scholars in the United States where he held full professorships at two prestigious institutions, Smith College and the University of California at San Diego, but no research and visiting fellowships elsewhere. Instead he was very much sought after in Europe. Thus he became a fellow at the Center for Interdisciplinary Research at Bielefeld University in 1986–1987 and at the Historical Commission in Berlin from 1989 to 1991. Two years later, he acted as Associate Director of Studies at the École des hautes études en sciences sociales in Paris and was given another fellowship at the Centro Studi Ligure in Bogliasco, Italy, in 1996–1997. It must be added that he received summer research grants from the Rockefeller Foundation, the American Philosophical Society, the National Endowment for the Humanities, and the Fulbright Commission, but also from the German Academic Exchange Service, the Thyssen Foundation, the French government, and the German Marshall Fund.

Since, apart from numerous articles and reviews, he published more than a dozen monographs and edited or co-edited three anthologies, his scholarly output is impressive enough to warrant a more detailed assessment of his work. What follows is a retrospective appreciation, designed to transcend Allan's all too self-conscious self-definition mentioned above and to put him back into the mainstream of American historical writing on modern Europe.

Allan's Scottish-born parents were first generation immigrants who settled in Kentucky. His father was a craftsman with a commuting job, and so his mother took their son every Friday to the Ashland railroad station to meet Mitchell senior. Eventually, the family became sufficiently prosperous to send their son to Davidson College from where he graduated with a B.A. in 1954. Subsequently he studied for an M.A. at Duke University and received another M.A. at Middlebury College in 1958. A Phi Beta Kappa student and highly motivated, he was accepted by Harvard University where William Langer, the diplomatic historian, and H. Stuart Hughes took him under their wings. Hughes had made a name for himself in 1952 with a major study on Oswald Spengler, followed in 1958 by his seminal book on *Consciousness and Society: The Reorientation of European Social Thought, 1890–1930*. Inspired by Hughes's kind of intellectual history, Allan began to work on Kurt Eisner, the left-wing radical who, after the abdication of King Ludwig III of Bavaria in November 1918, had been elected minister president of the Bavarian "Free State" by the regional Workers' and Soldiers' Council. Faced with the chaos of the Revolution, Eisner tried to restore some sort of order until he was assassinated by Count Arco auf Valley, a right-wing extremist on the fringes of the anti-Semitic Thule Society. This biographical focus enabled Allan to finish his doctoral dissertation in three years, but he then expanded the manuscript into a broader study of the revolutionary upheavals in Bavaria and the origins of the short-lived Bolshevik republic that Eugen Leviné and others established in Munich until they were defeated by the Free Corps, paramilitary units that the Republican government in Berlin had raised to stop the Leninist revolutionaries.

Allan's *Revolution in Bavaria* had little time for the Bolsheviks in Munich. However, he saw in the positions that Eisner took up a possibility "to attain some stable compromise between the council and parliamentary systems." What Allan raised here was the notion of a third way that was also being promoted by some younger West German scholars in the 1960s and that challenged the notion current in West Germany after World War II, i.e., that there were only two ways out of the crisis: Bolshevism or a bourgeois republic forged by Friedrich Ebert and the Social Democrats with the support of the traditional Imperial elites. The latter proposal appeared doomed from the start because of its compromise structure. The critics of this interpretation asserted that, like Eisner, Ebert should and could have pursued a third way by relying on those elements of the Council movement that rejected revolution, but wanted more far-reaching democratic reforms. In other words, they highlighted the chance to form a broader, more genuinely democratic base for the new Weimar Republic, capable of stemming the pressure of the rapidly growing anti-Republican Right.

In the meantime Allan had discovered not only West Germany where he had spent some months at the University of Freiburg in 1954–1955, but also Paris where he had signed up with the Institut d'études politiques in 1958 and about which he published a retrospective in 2011: *Witnessing Europe: The Personal History of an American Abroad*. In the mid-sixties he abandoned Bavarian history and turned to Franco-German relations in the nineteenth century. With Langer having interested him in international history, he turned to research on Otto von Bismarck. However, the problem for him did not lie "so much in a preoccupation with statecraft as with a too narrow conception of it." It was not a matter of abandoning biography, nor did he think that "the insistence on the wonders to be wrought by a straight dosage of economic and social history" was the right path to take. Rather Allan was thinking of a combination of both political and economic history, and the testing grounds for this approach was to be Franco-German relations in the Bismarckian era.

His first foray into this field came in 1971 in the form of a slim 130-page volume, entitled *Bismarck and the French Nation, 1848–1890*. In many ways, this was still a more traditional analysis of Prusso-German policy towards France, with some linking of politics to financial and commercial developments. What was new about it and probably inspired by the work of Hans-Ulrich Wehler on Bismarckian Germany was the stress on the interdependence of foreign and domestic policy-making. It was only in his next book of 1979 on *The German Influence in France after 1870: The Formation of the French Republic* that he explicitly combined economic history with political history, focusing on both domestic and foreign policy. Though by now a full professor at San Diego, it is nevertheless quite endearing to read how Allan justified the origins of this book: "The relationship between France and Germany, their similarities and their differences is a theme that has fascinated me since my first experience of Europe." He then added: "Scarcely a decade after the Second World War nothing could have been more natural for a young American student than to perceive the two nations as variations of the same civilization." While in the 1970s this early Cold War period seemed to lie way back in the past, "the traces" of his earlier experiences of Europe remained, and in this sense the book was "autobiographical." However, there was also the glaring gap in our knowledge about late nineteenth-century German and French history. While there were many studies that briefly mentioned German influences on France, none had "drawn the subject together," as Allan now proposed to do.

Popular images of the Franco-German relationship after 1870 still tend to stress the bitter enmity between the two countries following the swift German victory over Napoleon III, the occupation of the northern *départements*, the annexation of Alsace-Lorraine, and the imposition of reparations. It was all about French "revanchism." To be sure, Allan acknowledged that the newly founded German Empire was superior militarily and politically, and that Bismarck knew how to use this to his advantage. But whatever the irreconcilable rhetoric in public, behind the scenes the French leadership was quietly negotiating with Berlin to mitigate the terms of the peace agreement and to gain concessions, while Bismarck and the Prussian military watched suspiciously whether Paris was secretly trying to change the military balance. So, with the French leadership living in fear of another German invasion, Bismarck wielded the big stick of warfare not merely in the well-known "War in Sight" crisis of 1875, but also on earlier occasions.

However illuminating Allan's discussion of the political relationship in the 1870s may be, his examination of financial and economic interactions are arguably even more so. Whoever is looking for information on the issue of French reparations payments to Germany or the raising of loans to refloat the French economy will greatly profit from the relevant sub-chapters. This includes the intriguing role of bankers. Among them Gerson von Bleichroeder played a crucial mediating role, after Allan had persuaded his colleague Fritz Stern, then researching his influential book on Bismarck and Bleichroeder, to let him see some of the private correspondence. Overall, this book, with its focus on German influences reaching across the Rhine, is still a rewarding read for anyone looking for information on political and financial-economic links, including telling statistical tables.

No less important, the volume was the first in a trilogy, at the end of which he hoped to provide a comprehensive study of France and the many influences that Germany exerted on its neighbor up to 1914. He realized this plan when in 1984 he published the second volume, entitled *Victors and Vanquished: The German Influence on Army and Church in France after 1870*. With the first volume intended to provide "the context within which the French army and the Catholic Church attempted to reconsolidate their prerogatives" after 1870, this second volume revolves around religious and military problems up to the "traumatic *terminus ad quem* in the Dreyfus Affair." It is not possible to go into the rich detail of individual chapters, all of them again based on careful research in the French and German archives. After all, the French defeat by the Germans stimulated reforms of practically every aspect of the French armed forces. The training of officers and soldiers was rethought; fortifications, railway supply systems, and military hardware were modernized, all in order to try to overcome a condition of inferiority vis-à-vis the eastern neighbor that the French leadership thought was unacceptable. The second half of the volume is devoted to the problem of religion and government relationships with the Catholic Church and the Vatican at the time when Bismarck was waging his own Kulturkampf against Catholicism in Germany.

On the French side, the struggle for the country's "soul" and the confrontation between social and political conservatives and Republicanism ultimately reached its climax in the Dreyfus Affair. This part also contains insightful sub-chapters on Jules Ferry's reform of primary and secondary education against the backdrop of what Allan called the "German Model." The same applies to higher education, a field in which Germany had also become a model to the United States. Even if the Republic was stabilized against its irredentist domestic opposition, there was still the dread of Germany, which was expressed in terms of "a desire to catch up" rather than a "compulsion for revenge." It is this French sense of being left behind economically and demographically that enabled him to build the bridge to the third volume of his trilogy.

It appeared in 1989 under the title *The Divided Path: German Influence on Social Reform in France after 1870* after, as he admitted, the complexities of the subject had occupied him "for the better part of two decades" because it revolved around the "social question," then ubiquitous in most of Europe. During the decade preceding this volume's publication many books on this question had appeared that he gratefully incorporated. But as before, Allan went into a large number of archives to produce what in terms of scope and depth is arguably the most impressive volume in the trilogy. Postulating that there were three waves of social reform, he goes back to the pre-1870s with its "puzzles of poverty" and well-known demographic crisis. With the rise of modern medicine and public health concerns, there is again the issue of French perceptions of the German Model, before Allan delves into the administration of social reform at the Parisian center all the way to the level of city governments, including the pressures they came under from the medical lobby.

The discussion of the second wave tackles the role of gender and the history of different groups of women. There are thoughtful sections on single women, working women, and prostitutes, as well as the rudimentary systems of maternal care and family assistance at their disposal, followed by an analysis of the development of the medical profession and public health. Looking beyond Paris, he shows the gaps that were filled all too unevenly between the center and the provinces when it came to the genesis of legislation and the implementation of proposed laws and regulations. Part II concludes with an examination of early labor relations, the beginnings of the socialist movement, and the role of owners and managers. Part III finally covers the funding of social reform and the conflicts over the collection of taxes and their redistribution into a class-stratified society. With the Bismarckian social reforms always standing as the backdrop and matrix of comparison, Allan deals with the tensions between solidarism and mutualism, followed by a very good chapter on the spread of tuberculosis—the disease of the poor—and how to combat it. Finally, he moves to the underlying ideological conflicts, the question of modern housing and the priorities to be given to women and their children.

In light of his essentially institutional approach and focus on influences exerted by Germany, this book does not take the "cultural turn" into daily-life history and popular culture that came along in the 1980s. In this respect Allan stayed quite firmly in the camp of the West German Bielefeld School of socio-economic history. Indeed, it was Wehler and Jürgen Kocka at Bielefeld University who integrated Allan into a major and well-funded research project that brought together a large number of historians and social scientists in a series of workshops and discussion groups for intensive debates at the Center for Interdisciplinary Research. Away from West Germany's metropolitan centers, this was a sort of paradise where participants spent their time thinking, arguing, and writing, accommodated in comfortable studios. The central theme that the Bielefeld enterprise addressed was the European bourgeoisie before World War I in an attempt to complement the many studies of the working class that had been produced ever since the rise in the 1950s of labor historians such as Edward P. Thompson and Eric Hobsbawm. The labors of the Bielefeld meeting were eventually published in German in three volumes, covering virtually every aspect of the history of the European bourgeoisie. In 1993 Allan, who had been among the international contingent of invitees, edited jointly with Kocka a translation of selected articles in one volume, entitled *Bourgeois Society in Nineteenth-Century Europe*. Beyond European-wide articles on the politics and socio-economic position of the middle classes, this English version contains insightful contributions on the bourgeoisie in Britain, France, and Germany, with a concluding section on the embourgeoisement of the Jewish minority, the "Italian *Borghesia*," the Hungarian middle classes, and finally, a "cultural turn" examination of "German *Bürgerlichkeit* after 1800: Culture as Symbolic Practice" by an anthropologist.

Allan's contacts with the Bielefeld School were important because they resulted in a shift in his research interests. Although he still saw himself as a historian of modern France and Germany, with his trilogy completed he felt it was time to leave behind his interest in German influences on post-1870 France and to take up Franco-German comparative history. He knew from the Bielefeld project that it is not enough to look for similarities and differences in a bilateral comparison. Rather, he needed a *tertium comparationis*, something like a matrix against which to hold the empirical material that he found in the archives. He brilliantly lived up to this challenge in his next book, *The Great Train Race: Railways and the Franco-German Rivalry, 1815–1914*, published in 2000 after years of research in often remote archives. Having agonized quite a lot over how to structure his comparison, he decided to look at the development of the railroad systems in France and Central Europe in three discreet periods. After recounting how the two countries had tackled the introduction and expansion of their railroads institutionally, technologically, geographically, and politico-militarily each within their own national borders, Allan then added, for each of the three periods, a third sub-chapter in which he weighed the similarities and differences that the two nations developed in the hope to draw a balance sheet at the end. From this he assessed which of the two nations had succeeded in gaining a tangible competitive advantage over the other in terms of the institutional, technological, military and political-legislative solutions that they adopted. His conclusion: As far as its infrastructure was concerned, Imperial Germany had won the strategic train race by 1914. And yet "despite their economic prowess in Central Europe and the commercial integration of their railroads on the Continent, German commanders felt themselves encircled and feared that the balance of military forces in a two-front war would soon tilt against them. Germany thus became the aggressor in the West, not because political circumstances necessitated that action," but because Germany's military strategy as reflected in the infamous Schlieffen Plan "posited it." Allan's book therefore makes a pioneering contribution to the history not only of the rise of railroads in two modern European societies, but also of the origins of World War I.

It seems that this book, whose Epilogue makes the connection "From Trains to Trenches," encouraged Allan to advance into the first half of the twentieth century. If France's strategic inferiority had become a trauma before 1914, the defeat at the hands of Nazi Germany in 1940 was even more shattering. This further shift in his work probably also contributed to a change of heart that explains the subject matter of the books he wrote during the last years of his life. If hitherto he had been fairly balanced in his elective affinities towards France and Germany, the scales now tilted decidedly towards the French side. Accepting that there was something "peculiar" about the development of German society in the twentieth century that produced the Nazi dictatorship and the Holocaust, he decided, first of all, to undertake a short stock-taking exercise of his earlier work—in a book he called *A Stranger in Paris*, published in 2006. Here Allan insisted that the Franco-German relationship between 1870 and 1940 was fundamental to an understanding of modern European history. Yet there was no happy ending. In this book, with a cover showing a photograph of Hitler in front of the Eiffel Tower, Allan concluded: "The stranger, who had for so long remained a crucial part of French public life, thus returned to Paris in triumph, as the Third Republic came to its dolorous end." And having moved so explicitly into World War II, it was only logical that he should write his next gripping book on the German occupation of France in World War II.

This book, published in 2008 under the title of *Nazi Paris*, is in some ways a return to his earlier studies of the German impact on France, but, given the record of the Occupation, it rightly tells a very depressing story. By now close to age 75, Allan went off to the archives again and unearthed large amounts of material not just on the well-known topic of the treatment of the Jewish population and the Resistance in Paris, but also on the daily humiliations and reprisals that ordinary Parisians had to endure at the hands of the Germans. To be sure, there are also accounts of collaboration and abject callousness among the French bureaucracy, the police, businessmen, and intellectuals. But this book has justifiably received much praise not merely because of the many illuminating details it contains, but also because of its uncompromising condemnation of German policies.

If *Nazi Paris* is still set in the larger analytical frame that marked Allan's earlier studies, his attention now turned to individual experiences and biography. In the course of his research on Paris, he had learned about the availability of the journals and personal papers of Ernst Jünger, material that covered the period of his life in Paris during the war. Since so much had been written about Jünger's earlier life and politics, Allan decided to concentrate on the biographical sources, now held at the *Literaturarchiv* in Marbach. It is not a pretty picture that emerges from *The Devil's Captain*, considering that Jünger was aware of the murder of hostages, of SS torture, and of the deportation of the Jews from Drancy and other railroad terminals. On a trip to the Caucasus, moreover, Jünger learned about the horrendous atrocities that were being committed by the SS and the Wehrmacht in the East. Back in Paris, all this distressing information seems to have induced insomnia in Jünger at night as well as nervousness during the day when he participated in the display of Nazi power in parades along the Champs-Elysées and witnessed soldiers posing as arrogant bully boys on the boulevards. At the same time, he remained icy-cold in his outward demeanor. He socialized in bars and cafés, as if he were surrounded by a civilian society at peace, and had at least one serious love affair, while his wife and son were left behind in Hannover.

In short, it is difficult to warm to this devil's captain, and this may also explain why Allan was reluctant to spend more time on Jünger's actions towards the end of the Occupation and to make sense of his behavior then. He avers that the officer refused to join the conservative German resistance when one of the men involved in the July 1944 plot to assassinate Hitler tried to recruit him, though he had responded positively when in 1943 Hans Speidel, a close friend and superior at the Wehrmacht headquarters in Paris, encouraged him to write a memorandum. Entitled "Der Friede," it was apparently to be published after a successful coup. The coup failed; but how is one to interpret Jünger's actions that could have cost him his life if the document had been discovered by the Gestapo? Jünger published "Der Friede" after the war, dedicating it to his only son Ernstel, killed in action in the final months of the war. In short, this mourning father needs further study than Allan provided in his book, also in light of Jünger's extremely negative public image in early postwar Germany. People remembered all too well his political connections to the anti-Republican Stahlhelm veterans association and his contacts with Hitler. Disgruntled but unwilling to admit the errors of his ways, he retreated to Wilflingen near Stuttgart to tend his garden and collections of insects and to write esoteric novels that never became part of the canon of postwar West German literature. In his quest to promote Franco-German reconciliation, Chancellor Helmut Kohl invited Jünger to join him with French president François Mitterrand—the two leaders holding hands on the battlefield of World War I where Jünger had once received his baptism of fire.

Pursuing his latest interest in biography, Allan published three more books between 2011 and 2016. The most detailed one, published in 2016 and entitled *The Unrepentant Patriot*, is a biography of the German dramatist Carl Zuckmayer, narrating his success during the Weimar Republic, his flight from the Nazis to Vermont, and his return to Europe after 1945. For Allan this book was a sequel to *The Devil's Captain*, as he had always been mesmerized by Zuckmayer after he had published his drama *The Devil's General*, the story of Admiral Wilhelm Canaris, the head of the Abwehr, the Wehrmacht intelligence arm, and his intellectual journey from his service under Hitler to his covert support of the anti-Nazi resistance. The other book, *Fleeing Nazi Germany: Five Historians Migrate to America* (2011), contains vignettes on refugee historians whom Allan met during his long academic career: Felix Gilbert, Klemens von Klemperer, Werner T. Angress, Peter Gay, and Fritz Stern. In between he wrote *Socialism and the Emergence of the Welfare State*, in which he went back to the themes of the last volume of his trilogy in part to tell an American readership about the European traditions of social justice when US-President Obama's efforts to help the underprivileged and uninsured were under siege.

This being a Memorial written for an academic journal, Allan's personal and family life can only be mentioned in passing. But it should not be forgotten that, after his marriage fell apart, he raised his two daughters as a single parent and, as may be gleaned from the fact that he dedicated several of his books to Catherine and Alexandra, his daughters were very close to him until his final hours. He also kept and nurtured many friendships all over the world. In the first volume of his trilogy, Allan expressed the hope that those three books would "add to a comprehensive understanding of the early years of the Third Republic and also provide a basis for further study of the Franco-German confrontation that has dominated Western Europe ever since." Although his work deserved greater recognition during his life-time, it is to be hoped that its central importance to modern European history will continue be recognized and cited now that he is no longer with us.

*Reprinted with permission from *French Politics, Culture & Society*, 36 (1), pp. 148–57.

Volker Berghahn is the Seth Low Emeritus Professor of History at Columbia University. He taught at the universities of East Anglia and Warwick in the UK before moving to Brown University in 1988 and to Columbia in 1998. He has published some twenty books on modern German History, European-American cultural and business relations, and Historiography, including *Modern Germany: Society, Economy and Politics in the 20th Century* (1987); *American Big Business in Britain and Germany: A Comparative Analysis of Two 'Special Relationships' in the 20th Century* (2014); and *Between Hitler and Adenauer: Journalists and the Moral Reconstruction of West Germany* (2018).

ABBREVIATIONS

BA	Bundesarchiv, Koblenz
DLA	Deutsches Literaturarchiv, Marbach am Neckar
ECPA	Établissement Cinématographique et Photographique de l'Armée, Ivry-sur-Seine
MBF	Mititärbefehlshaber in Frankreich
NATO	North Atlantic Treaty Organization
NSDAP	Nationalsozialistische Deutsche Arbeiterpartei
OKW	Oberkommando der Wehrmacht
SS	Schutzstaffel
SW	*Sämtliche Werke*

NOTES

Introduction

1. Ernst Jünger, "Kirchhorster Blätter," 14 November 1944, *Sämtliche Werke* [hereafter cited as *SW*], 18 vols. and 4 supplementary vols. (Stuttgart, 1978–2003), 3: p. 330.
2. See Eva Dempewolf, *Blut und Tinte. Eine Interpretation der verschiedenen Fassungen von Ernst Jüngers Kriegstagebüchern vor dem politischen Hintergrund der Jahre 1920 bis 1981* (Würzburg, 1992); and John King, *"Wann hat dieser Scheisskrieg ein Ende?" Writing and Rewriting the First World War* (Schnellroda, 2003).
3. The most capable such investigation to date is the unpublished *Magisterarbeit* at the Humboldt University, Berlin, by Felix Krömer, "Offizier und Tagebuchautor im besetzten Paris. Die Darstellung des NS-Regimes in Ernst Jüngers Journalen 1941–1944," (2004). His principal findings are summarized by Krömer, "Die Handschriften von Ernst Jüngers Pariser Tagebüchern—stereoskopisch betrachtet," *Zeitschrift für Germanistik*, Neue Folge 2 (2005): pp. 337–51. On the frequent use of pseudonyms by Jünger, see especially Tobias Wimbauer, *Personenregister der Tagebücher Ernst Jüngers* (2nd ed.; Schnellroda, 2003).
4. Peter de Mendelssohn, *Der Geist in der Despotie: Versuche über die moralischen Möglichkeiten des Intellektuellen in der totalitären Gesellschaft* (Berlin, 1953); Karl-Heinz Bohrer, *Die Ästhetik des Schreckens: Die pessimistische Romantik und Ernst Jüngers Frühwerk* (Munich and Vienna, 1978).
5. Kurt Sontheimer, *Antidemokratisches Denken in der Weimarer Republik: Die politischen Ideen des deutschen Nationalismus zwischen 1918 und 1933* (Munich, 1962); Hans-Peter Schwarz, *Der konservative Anarchist: Politik und Zeitkritik Ernst Jüngers* (Freiburg im Breisgau, 1962). Similar in approach is an analysis of Jünger's ephemeral but indicative affiliation with a conservative veteran's organization by Volker R. Berghahn, *Der Stahlhelm. Bund der Frontsoldaten 1918–1935* (Düsseldorf, 1966).
6. Martin Meyer, *Ernst Jünger* (Munich, 1990); Paul Noack, *Ernst Jünger: eine Biographie* (Berlin, 1998); Steffen Martus, *Ernst Jünger* (Stuttgart and Weimar, 2001).
7. Heimo Schwilk, *Ernst Jünger: Ein Jahrhundertleben* (Munich and Zurich, 2007); Helmuth Kiesel, *Ernst Jünger. Die Biographie* (Munich, 2007).

8. See the up-to-date analysis by Kiesel, "Tendenzen der publistischen und wissentschaftlichen Auseinandersetzung mit Ernst Jünger und seinem Werk," in Natalia Zarska, Gerald Diesner, and Wojciech Kunicki (eds.), *Ernst Jünger – eine Bilanz* (Leipzig, 2010), pp. 512–19.

9. Marcus Paul Bullock, *The Violent Eye: Ernst Jünger's Visions and Revisions on the European Right* (Detroit, 1992).

10. Elliot Y. Neaman, *A Dubious Past: Ernst Jünger and the Politics of Literature after Nazism* (Berkeley, Los Angeles, and London, 1999). Neaman has trouble with names, places, and dates. For example, he writes "René Bosquet" (Bousquet); "Henri de Montherlant" (Henry); "Alain de Benoist-Mechin" (Jacques Benoist-Méchin); "Marcel Deat" (Déat); "Hans Ullrich Wehler" (Hans-Ulrich); "Helmut Kiesel" (Helmuth); "Freiburg in Breisgau" (im); "Avenue de Kleber" (Avenue Kléber); during the war Jünger took up his censorship duties in Paris on "July 24, 1940" (April 24, 1941); Jünger celebrated his sixtieth birthday on "March 27, 1955" (March 29).

11. Thomas Nevin, *Ernst Jünger and Germany: Into the Abyss, 1914–1945* (Durham, NC, 1996).

12. Klemens von Klemperer, *Germany's New Conservatism: Its History and Dilemma in the Twentieth Century* (Princeton, 1957), p. 188; Dagmar Barnouw, *Weimar Intellectuals and the Threat of Modernity* (Bloomington and Indianapolis, 1988).

13. It is noteworthy, and symptomatic of the regard with which Jünger is viewed in France, that a two-volume set of his translated writings and journals concerning the two world wars has recently been issued in the prestigious Pléiade series. Astutely edited, the annotations in these tomes are full of useful explanations, a remarkable (but still controversial) tribute to a foreign author by French scholarship. Julien Hervier et al. (eds.), *Ernst Jünger: Journaux de guerre* (2 vols.; Paris, 2008). See also Danièlle Beltran-Vidal, "Die Rezeption Jüngers in Frankreich," in Zarsak et al. (eds.), *Ernst Jünger – eine Bilanz*, pp. 310–20.

14. See Allan Mitchell, *Nazi Paris: The History of an Occupation, 1940–1944* (New York and Oxford, 2008).

Chapter 1

1. Schwilk, *Ernst Jünger*, p. 53. On Jünger's school years in general, see ibid., pp. 20–65; and Kiesel, *Ernst Jünger*, pp. 22–56.

2. "How far his understanding went of the books read—for instance, the writings of Schopenhauer—and how Jünger absorbed these extremely different readings cannot be determined in detail," observes Kiesel, *Ernst Jünger*, p. 43.

3. Ibid., pp. 45–49; and Schwilk, *Ernst Jünger*, pp. 61–65.

4. Jünger, "Kriegsausbruch 1914," SW 1: p. 543. See Kiesel, *Ernst Jünger*, pp. 49–54; and Schwilk, *Ernst Jünger*, pp. 82–89.

5. See Kiesel, *Ernst Jünger*, pp. 110–19; and Schwilk, *Ernst Jünger*, pp. 92–113.

6. See Kiesel, *Ernst Jünger*, p. 121; and Schwilk, *Ernst Jünger*, pp. 116–21.

7. Jünger commented on his purpose: "A journal has no theme; it scarcely has a form. It is intended to capture the first fleeting contact with reality and its impression. Therein lies its limitation and its fascination." Jünger, "Erste Fassung," 12 August 1958, Sammlung des Coudres, DLA Marbach. See Kiesel, *Ernst Jünger*, pp. 123–27; Schwilk, *Ernst Jünger*, pp. 121–98; and Neaman, *A Dubious Past*, p. 26. Estimates of Jünger's

wounds run as high as fourteen, although only seven are recorded in his military credentials (*Wehrpass*), conserved at the Deutsches Literaturarchiv (DLA) in Marbach.

8. After *In Stahlgewittern,* Jünger continued to present his war experience in *Feuer und Blut, Das Wäldchen 125,* and *Der Kampf als inneres Erlebnis.* On these, see Martus, *Ernst Jünger,* pp. 32–48. On "Ernst Jüngers Frühwerk und das Kriegserlebnis," see also Hans-Harald Müller, *Der Krieg und die Schriftsteller. Der Kriegsroman der Weimarer Republik* (Stuttgart,1986), pp. 211–95.

9. Jünger's connection with Spengler is emphasized by Georg Lukács, *Die Zerstörung der Vernunft* (Neuwied am Rhein and Berlin, 1962), p. 463; Meyer, *Ernst Jünger,* pp. 163–76; and Schwarz, *Der konservative Anarchist,* pp. 76–83. See also Johannes Volmert, *Ernst Jünger:"In Stahlgewittern"* (Munich, 1985); Ulrich Böhme, *Fassungen bei Ernst Jünger* (Meisenhaim, 1972), pp. 7–52; Milan Hornacek, "Der Sprachbegriff der konservativen Revolution im Frühwerk Ernst Jüngers (1920-1934)," in Zarska et al. (eds.), *Ernst Jünger—eine Bilanz,* pp. 112–29; Kiesel, *Ernst Jünger,* pp. 138–42, 172–229; and Schwilk, *Ernst Jünger,* pp. 200–208.

10. See Kiesel, *Ernst Jünger,* pp. 166–72; and Schwilk, *Ernst Jünger,* pp. 210–22, 252–54.

11. Jünger's comportment at home was described by his spouse: "In this clear, morally impressed picture eroticism is lacking as a nurturing and giving force, as a powerful inundating stream. … With priestly strictness he constructs barriers and dams against himself." Gretha von Jeinsen, *Silhouetten. Eigenwillige Betrachtungen* (Pfullingen, 1955), pp.187–88.

12. Schwilk, *Ernst Jünger,* p. 209. See also, Harro Segeberg, "Revolutionärer Nationalismus. Ernst Jünger während der Weimarer Republik," in Helmut Scheuer (ed.), *Dichter und ihre Nation* (Frankfurt a. M., 1993), pp. 327–42.

13. First published in daily installments (11–27 April 1923) in the *Hannoverschen Kurier, Sturm* did not appear in book form until 1963, when it was rediscovered and edited by Hans Peter des Coudres. See Schwilk, *Ernst Jünger. Leben und Werk in Bildern und Texten* (Stuttgart, 1988), pp. 79–138; King, "Wann hat dieser Scheisskrieg ein Ende?," pp. 221–45; and Barnouw, *Weimar Intellectuals,* pp. 207–11.

14. See Kiesel, *Ernst Jünger,* pp. 238–50; and Schwilk, *Ernst Jünger,* pp. 254–60.

15. Yet Spengler had an objection: "Like many others, you have not been able to free the concept of worker from Marxist phraseology." Spengler to Jünger, 25 September 1932, A-Jünger, DLA Marbach. See Horst Mühleisen, *Ernst Jünger in Berlin, 1927–1933* (Frankfurt an der Oder, 1998); Michael Jaeger, "Die Gestalt der Moderne. Ernst Jüngers Arbeiter," in Zarska et al. (eds.), *Ernst Jünger—eine Bilanz,* pp. 46–56; Kiesel, *Ernst Jünger,* pp. 266–74; and Schwilk, *Ernst Jünger,* pp. 273–76, 352–56, 384–99. "This book was virtually stillborn. … It is a work he would perhaps sooner have forgotten," remarks Nevin, *Ernst Jünger and Germany,* pp. 115–40.

16. A second version was published in 1938. Jünger, *Das abenteuerliche Herz. Zweite Fassung* (Stuttgart, 1979). See Martus, *Ernst Jünger,* pp. 72–77.

17. Cited by Schwilk, *Ernst Jünger,* p. 325. See ibid., pp. 298–300, 306–330; and Kiesel, *Ernst Jünger,* pp. 317–35, 344–67.

18. Letter from Jünger to Ludwig Alwens, 5 April 1933, cited by Kiesel, *Ernst Jünger,* p. 408.

19. Among others, Bohrer claims that Jünger's views perceptibly evolved during the Weimar Republic. That thesis is sharply rejected, and Jünger is charged with simply

wallowing in a "conceptual muddle," by Barnouw, *Weimar Intellectuals*, pp. 194–230. See Lothar Bluhm, "Ernst Jünger als Tagebuchautor und die 'Innere Emigration,'" in Hans-Harold Müller and Harro Segeberg (eds.), *Ernst Jünger im 20. Jahrhundert* (Munich, 1995), pp. 125–53.

20. See Kiesel, *Ernst Jünger*, pp. 423–58; and Schwilk, *Ernst Jünger*, pp. 360–74.

21. *Auf den Marmorklippen* "allows a variety of interpretations, of which that of an allegorical satire is only one," concludes Mendelssohn, *Der Geist in der Despotie*, pp. 184–87. See Barnouw, *Weimar Intellectuals*, pp. 221–30; Kiesel, *Ernst Jünger*, pp. 458–81; and Schwilk, *Ernst Jünger*, pp. 375–79.

Chapter 2

1. The period from 1 September 1939 to 24 April 1941 is covered very hastily by Kiesel, *Ernst Jünger*, pp. 486–93; and by Schwilk, *Ernst Jünger*, pp. 379–81.

2. Jünger, "Gärten und Strassen," 30 August 1939–17 March 1940, *SW* 2: pp. 68–116.

3. Ibid., 28–29 March 1940, *SW* 2: pp. 116–21.

4. Ibid., 16–23 April, 8 May 1940, *SW* 2: pp. 127–32.

5. Ibid., 10 May 1940, *SW* 2: pp. 132–33.

6. Ibid., 17–26 May 1940, *SW* 2: pp. 135–45.

7. Ibid., 27 May–2 June 1940, *SW* 2: pp. 145–53. See Julian Jackson, *France. The Dark Years 1940–1944* (Oxford, 2001), p. 273.

8. Jünger, "Gärten und Strassen," 3–6 June 1940, *SW* 2: pp. 153–57.

9. Ibid., 7–15 June 1940, *SW* 2: pp. 157–72.

10. Ibid., 16–18 June 1940, *SW* 2: pp. 172–79. See Stanley Hoffmann, "Le Trauma de 1940," in Jean-Pierre Azéma and François Bédarida (eds.), *La France des années noires* (2 vols.; Paris, 1993), 1: pp. 131–50.

11. Jünger, "Gärten und Strassen," 21 June 1940, *SW* 2: p. 184.

12. Ibid., 22–24 June 1940, *SW* 2: pp. 185–90.

13. Ibid., 27 June–2 July 1940, *SW* 2: pp. 195–98.

14. Ibid., 3–24 July 1940, *SW* 2: pp. 199–221. "*Es ist die einzige Stadt, zu der ich ein Verhältnis besitze wie zu einer Frau.*" This quotation appears in a letter from Jünger to Carl Schmitt, 28 June 1941, cited by Schwilk, *Ernst Jünger*, p. 381.

15. See Kiesel, *Ernst Jünger*, p. 375; and Ulrich Herbert, *Best. Biographische Studien über Radikalismus, Weltanschauung und Vernunft, 1903–1989* (Bonn, 1996), pp. 88–109. Jünger and Best had been acquainted since 1925, notes Dominique Venner, *Histoire de la Collaboration* (Paris, 2000), p. 148.

16. Jünger, "Das Erste Pariser Tagebuch," 18 February–6 April 1941, *SW* 2: pp. 225–32.

Chapter 3

1. Jünger, "Das Erste Pariser Tagebuch," pp. 24–27 April 1941, *SW* 2: pp. 233–36.

2. Ibid., 29 April–1 May 1941, *SW* 2: pp. 236–38. Just for the record, the correct name is Brasserie La Lorraine, but Jünger repeatedly refers in his journals to the "Brasserie Lorraine."

3. Ibid., 3–11 May 1941, *SW* 2: pp. 238–39.
4. Ibid., 20–24 May 1941, *SW* 2: pp. 241–42.
5. Ibid. On his impressions of Jünger, see Hans Speidel, *Aus unserer Zeit. Erinnerungen* (Berlin, Frankfurt a. M., and Vienna, 1971), pp. 109–12. A very flattering sketch of Speidel is offered by Walter Bargatzky, *Hotel Majestic. Ein Deutscher im besetzten Frankreich* (Freiburg, Basel, and Vienna, 1987), pp. 46–47.
6. Jünger, "Das Erste Pariser Tagebuch," 29 May 1941, *SW* 2: pp. 244–47. See Krömer, "Die Handschriften von Ernst Jüngers Pariser Tagebüchern," pp. 345–47.
7. Jünger, "Das Erste Pariser Tagebuch," 30 May 1941, *SW* 2: p. 247.
8. Ibid., 3, 8, 14 June 1941, *SW* 2: pp. 248–52.
9. Ibid., 24 June 1941, *SW* 2: p. 256. See Mitchell, *Nazi Paris*, pp. 47–48. A recent useful overview of Franco-German collaboration during the war years is also provided by Mark Mazower, *Hitler's Empire: How the Nazis Ruled Europe* (New York, 2008), pp. 416–45.
10. On Jünger's official duties in the Abteilung Ic of the German Kommandostab in Paris, see Hans Umbreit, *Der Militärbefehlshaber in Frankreich 1940–1944* (Boppard, 1968), pp. 21–22. On Best's role in the military administration, see Ahlrich Meyer, *Die deutsche Besatzung in Frankreich 1940–1944. Widerstandsbekämpfung und Judenverfolgung* (Darmstadt, 2000), pp. 13–33.
11. Jünger, "Das Erste Pariser Tagebuch," 25 June 1941, *SW* 2: pp. 256–57.
12. Ibid., 5, 12 July 1941, *SW* 2: pp. 258–59. "Morris" was almost certainly an American journalist who corresponded after the war from Famersville, Texas, to relate that he had written two reviews of Jünger's work for a Kansas City newspaper. Morris Horton to Jünger, 27 April 1951, A-Jünger, DLA Marbach. There is speculation that "Mme. Scrittore" was actually a pseudonym for Florence Gould. See Wimbauer, *Personenregister*, p. 118.
13. Jünger, "Das Erste Pariser Tagebuch," 8 October 1941, *SW* 2: p. 260.
14. See Mitchell, *Nazi Paris*, pp. 47–54.
15. Jünger, "Das Erste Pariser Tagebuch," 8 October 1941, *SW* 2: pp. 260–61. See Philippe Burrin, *La France à l'heure allemande 1941–1944* (Paris, 1995), p. 209.
16. Jünger, "Das Erste Pariser Tagebuch," 11 October, 23 November, 4 December 1941, 10 January 1942, *SW* 2: pp. 261–80, 289. See Jackson, *France: The Dark Years*, p. 311. On Jünger and Gallimard, see Burrin, *La France à l'heure allemande*, pp. 335–38; and Gisèle Sapiro, "La collaboration littéraire," in Albrecht Betz and Stefan Martens (eds.), *Les intellectuels et l'Occupation, 1940–1944. Collaborer, partir, résister* (Paris, 2004), pp. 39–63.
17. Jünger, "Das Erste Pariser Tagebuch," 19 July, 14 October 1941, *SW* 2: pp. 259–63. See Margot Traureck, *Friedrich Sieburg in Frankreich. Seine literarisch-publizistischen Stellungnahmen zwischen den Weltkriegen in Vergleich mit Positionen Ernst Jüngers* (Heidelberg, 1987), pp. 111–30.
18. For further details, see the Postscript.
19. Jünger, "Das Erste Pariser Tagebuch," 21, 23 October, 19 November, 3 December 1941, *SW* 2: pp. 266–67, 275, 278–79. See Wimbauer, *Personenregister*, p. 251, who gives one of these pseudonyms as "Mme. Armenonville"; but Sophie, in signing a card in 1944, clearly writes "Armenoville." Sophie Ravoux to Jünger, 16 August 1944, A-Jünger, DLA Marbach. See also Kiesel, *Ernst Jünger*, pp. 503–509; and Krömer, "Die Handschriften von Ernst Jüngers Pariser Tagebüchern," pp. 343–45.

20. Jünger, "Das Erste Pariser Tagebuch," 22 October, 15 November 1941, *SW* 2: pp. 266, 273. On sexual mores and some of Jünger's flirtations in Paris, see Burrin, *La France à l'heure allemande*, pp. 210–14; and Richard Vinen, *The Unfree French: Life under the Occupation* (New Haven and London, 2006), pp. 168–69.

21. Warm thanks are due to Frau Dr. Liselotte Jünger for generously allowing me to review this correspondence. See the Postscript for further details.

22. Jünger, "Das Erste Pariser Tagebuch," 12 November 1941, *SW* 2: pp. 270–71.

23. Ibid., 24 December 1941, 2 January 1942, *SW* 2: pp. 283–85.

24. Ibid., 18 January, 1–3 February 1942, *SW* 2: pp. 292–93, 299–301. On Jünger and Cocteau with Marais, see Patrick Buisson, *1940–1945 Années érotiques. Vichy ou les infortunes da la vertu* (Paris, 2008), pp. 228–41.

25. Jünger, "Das Erste Pariser Tagebuch," 8 February 1942, *SW* 2: pp. 302–303.

26. Ibid., 23 February 1942, *SW* 2: pp. 308–309.

27. Ibid., 6 March 1942, *SW* 2: p. 315.

28. Ibid., 10 March 1942, *SW* 2: pp. 318–19. See also Heinrich Bücheler, *Carl-Heinrich von Stülpnagel. Soldat—Philosoph—Verschwörer* (Berlin and Frankfurt a. M., 1989), pp. 20–21, 250–51.

29. Jünger, "Das Erste Pariser Tagebuch," 12 March 1942, *SW* 2: p. 320. "Was Jünger anti-Semitic? Yes and No," writes Louis Dupeux: "He despised the biological anti-Semitism of the Nazis but shared their cultural animosity toward Jews." Dupeux, "Der 'neue Nationalismus' Ernst Jüngers 1925–1932. Vom heroischen Soldatentum zur politisch-metaphysischen Totalität," in Peter Koslowski (ed.), *Die grossen Jagden des Mythos. Ernst Jünger in Frankreich* (Munich, 1996), pp. 15–40.

30. Jünger, "Das Erste Pariser Tagebuch," 14, 16, 28 March 1942, *SW* 2: pp. 320–23. See the memoir by Gerhard Heller, *Un Allemand à Paris 1941–1944* (Paris, 1981), pp. 57–66; and Venner, *Histoire de la Collaboration*, p. 185.

31. Jünger, "Das Erste Pariser Tagebuch," 7–10 April 1942, *SW* 2: pp. 324–26. Speidel, *Aus unserer Zeit*, pp. 119–20.

32. Jünger, "Das Erste Pariser Tagebuch," 20, 24 May, 29 June, 4 July 1942, *SW* 2: pp. 330–32, 339, 341. See Buisson, *1940–1945 Années érotiques*, pp. 412–13.

33. Jünger, "Das Erste Pariser Tagebuch," 7, 14 June, 18 July 1942, *SW* 2: pp. 336–37, 347. See Mitchell, *Nazi Paris*, pp. 88–89.

34. Jünger, "Das Erste Pariser Tagebuch," 19 July 1942, *SW* 2: pp. 347–48.

35. Ibid., 22, 26 July 1942, *SW* 2: pp. 349–51, 355. Jünger also later visited the studio of Georges Braque. See Jackson, *France: The Dark Years*, pp. 302–303; and Hervier (ed.), *Ernst Jünger*, 1: p. 128.

36. Jünger, "Das Erste Pariser Tagebuch," 26 August 1942, *SW* 2: pp. 368–69.

37. Ibid., 16 August 192, *SW* 2: pp. 364–366.

38. Ibid., 26 August, 8, 18, 29 September 1942, *SW* 2: pp. 368, 373, 381–82, 384–85.

39. Ibid., 2, 7, 9 October 1942, *SW* 2: pp. 388–90, 396–97.

40. Ibid., 12–14 October 1942, *SW* 2: pp. 398–400.

41. Ibid., 15 October 1942, *SW* 2: pp. 401–405. Suffering from a lung ailment, Walter Bargatzky spent four months in the same clinic at Suresnes in early 1942. He, too, could see Mont Valérien from his room, from which he could also hear shots of the execution squads in operation there. Jünger makes no mention of such noise. Bargatzky, *Hotel Majestic*, pp. 90–91.

42. Jünger, "Das Erste Pariser Tagebuch," 23 October 1942, *SW* 2: p. 406.

Chapter 4

1. By one count, Jünger recorded eighteen dreams in "Gärten und Strassen" and forty-two in "Das Erste Pariser Tagebuch." Wolfgang Brandes, Der "Neue Stil" in Ernst Jüngers"Strahlungen" (Bonn, 1990), p. 31. See also Hervier, "Ernst Jünger: de l'histoire mythique à la surréalité concrète du rêve," in Nicole Pelletier et al. (eds.), L'Allemagne et la crise de la raison (Bordeaux, 2001), pp. 99–111.

2. Jünger, "Das Erste Pariser Tagebuch," 28 March 1942, SW 2: p. 322. Later he confessed: "It is sometimes difficult for me to distinguish between my conscious and unconscious existence." Ibid., 26 August 1942, SW 2: p. 369.

3. Jünger, "Gärten und Strassen," 12 April, 3 July, 16 August 1939, 10, 31 May 1940, SW 2: pp. 35–36, 58, 66, 132, 151; and "Das Erste Pariser Tagebuch," 12 April 1941, 10 August 1942, SW 2: pp. 232, 362.

4. Jünger, "Gärten und Strassen," 19 June, 8 July 1940, SW 2: pp. 179, 203. There are many examples of dreams of his father: e.g., "Das Erste Pariser Tagebuch," 18 June, 8 December, 24 December 1941, 10 January, 13 October 1942, SW 2: pp. 255, 282–84, 398–99.

5. Ibid., 12 April 1941, 13 August 1942, SW 2: pp. 232–33, 363.

6. Jünger, "Gärten und Strassen," 21 September 1939, 2 February 1940, SW 2: pp. 73, 98; and "Das Erste Pariser Tagebuch," 10, 24 December 1941, 23 February 1942, SW 2: pp. 283–84, 310.

7. Ibid., 29 June, 9 July 1942, SW 2: pp. 339, 344.

8. Ibid., 18 July, 10, 12, 28 August, 23 September, 13–15 October 1942, SW 2: pp. 347, 362–63, 370, 382, 398–401.

9. About making entries into his journal, Jünger later said: "It was like daily plucking an apple from a tree. It is not necessary to understand the tree as a whole." Quoted by Hervier, Entretiens avec Ernst Jünger (Paris, 1986), p. 114.

10. Jünger, "Das Erste Pariser Tagebuch," 6 June 1942, SW 2: p. 335.

11. Jünger, "Gärten und Strassen," 19 May, 23 July 1939, SW 2: pp. 49, 63.

12. Jünger, "Das Erste Pariser Tagebuch," 8 September 1942, SW 2: p. 372. See Kiesel, Ernst Jünger, pp. 233–38, 262–63; and Jeffrey Herf, Reactionary Modernism: Technology, Culture, and Politics in Weimar and the Third Reich (Cambridge, 1984), pp. 70–108.

13. Jünger, "Das Erste Pariser Tagebuch," 15 September 1942, SW 2: p. 376. "It may be noted that, with the experience of Nazism, Jünger's rather benevolent religious neutrality begins to transform into frank sympathy," observes Hervier (ed.), Ernst Jünger, p. xii. See Schwilk, Ernst Jünger, pp. 69–72.

14. Jünger, "Gärten und Strassen," 18 January 1940, SW 2: p. 95.

15. Ibid., 3 November 1939, 29–30 January 1940, SW 2: pp. 77–78, 97.

16. Jünger, "Das Erste Pariser Tagebuch," 8 December 1941, 23 February 1942, SW 2: pp. 282, 308. See Sven Olaf Berggötz, "Ernst Jünger und die Geiseln. Die Denkschrift von Ernst Jünger über die Geiselerschiessungen in Frankreich 1941/42," Vierteljahrsheft für Zeitgeschichte 51 (2003): pp. 405–72. This piece contains the text of Jünger's long memorandum, "Zur Geiselfrage. Schilderung der Fälle und ihrer Auswirkungen" (pp. 418–57), as well as his German translation of thirty-four final letters written by condemned French hostages (pp. 457–72).

17. Jünger, "Das Erste Pariser Tagebuch," 22 February 1942, SW 2: p. 307.

18. Ibid., 2 July 1942, SW 2: pp. 340–41.

19. In his Paris journals Jünger made frequent references to an extended essay to be called "Der Friede." Originally conceived as a magnanimous call for European youth to unite under a victorious German Reich, it became instead a supplication for mercy after its defeat. This exercise thus proved to be frustrating and finally abortive. See Gérard Schneilin, "Betrachtungen zu Ernst Jüngers Pariser Tagebüchern," in Koslowski (ed.), *Die grossen Jagden des Mythos*, pp. 64–78; Hervier (ed.), *Ernst Jünger*, 2: pp. 1185–88; and Gerhard Loose, "Zur Entstehungsgeschichte von Ernst Jüngers Schrift 'Der Friede,'" *Modern Language Notes* 74 (1959), pp. 51–58.

Chapter 5

1. Jünger, "Kaukasische Aufzeichnungen," 24 October–10 November 1942, *SW* 2: pp. 409–13. See Mitchell, *Nazi Paris*, pp. 93–99.
2. Jünger, "Kaukasische Aufzeichnungen," 12–23 November 1942, *SW* 2: pp. 413–22.
3. Ibid., 25 November 1942, *SW* 2: pp. 423–24.
4. Ibid., 27 November–7 December 1942, *SW* 2: pp. 425–35.
5. Ibid., 10–12, 18 December 1942, *SW* 2: pp. 437–42, 453.
6. Ibid., 14, 21 December 1942, *SW* 2: pp. 445–48, 456–59.
7. Ibid., 22–24 December 1942, *SW* 2: pp. 460–64.
8. Ibid., 24, 31 December 1942, *SW* 2: pp. 463, 468–69.
9. Ibid., 31 December 1942, *SW* 2: p. 470.
10. Ibid., 1 January 1943, *SW* 2: pp. 471–72.
11. Ibid., 2 January 1943, *SW* 2: pp. 472–73.
12. Ibid., 6–8, 21 January 1943, *SW* 2: pp. 478–86.
13. Ibid., 24 January, 10–14 February 1943, *SW* 2: pp. 487, 489–91; and Jünger, "Das Zweite Pariser Tagebuch," 19 February 1943, *SW* 3: pp. 11–12.

Chapter 6

1. Jünger, "Die Hütte im Weinberg," 29 March 1946, *SW* 3: p. 610. See Schwilk, *Ernst Jünger*, pp. 262–66; and Kiesel, *Ernst Jünger*, pp. 266–74.
2. Hitler to Jünger, 27 May 1926, A-Jünger, DLA Marbach. Hess to Jünger, 11 June 1926, ibid. Goebbels to Jünger, 10 May 1927, ibid. Jünger also saw Otto Strasser "frequently." Jünger to Armin Mohler, 28 February 1954, ibid. See Berghahn, *Der Stahlhelm*; and Kiesel, *Ernst Jünger*, pp. 280–92.
3. Jünger, "Schlusswort zu einem Aufsatze," (first published in *Widerstand* in January 1930); and "Über Nationalismus und Judenfrage," (first published in the *Süddeutsche Monatshefte* in September 1930), in Sven Olaf Berggötz (ed.), *Ernst Jünger: Politische Publizistik 1919-1933* (Stuttgart, 2001), pp. 538–46, 587–92. On Jünger's relation to National Socialism, see the commentary of Berggötz, ibid., pp. 854–61. See also Kiesel, *Ernst Jünger*, pp. 303–17; Schwilk, *Ernst Jünger*, pp. 289–91; and the section on "Der heroische Nationalismus bei Ernst Jünger" by Sontheimer, *Antidemokratisches Denken in der Weimarer Republik*, pp. 128–32.
4. "Rundrufe vom 17.11.1933, Anweisung Nr. 63," 17 November 1933, A-Jünger, DLA Marbach. See Kiesel, *Ernst Jünger*, pp. 339–44; and Schwilk, *Ernst Jünger*, pp. 340–62. On the exchange of writings between Jünger and Hitler, see also Timothy W.

Ryback, *Hitler's Private Library:The Books that Shaped His Life* (New York, 2009), pp. 80–84.

5. Jünger, "Gärten und Strassen," 28 April 1939, *SW* 2: pp. 42–43. See Schwilk, *Ernst Jünger*, pp. 374–75.

6. Jünger, "Das Erste Pariser Tagebuch," 26 June 1941, *SW* 2: p. 257.

7. Ibid., 25 October 1941, *SW* 2: p. 268.

8. Ibid., 13, 18 January, 8, 23 February 1942, *SW* 2: pp. 290, 292, 302–303, 310. In those evening gatherings, "we spoke very freely about the evolution of the military and political situation," recalled Heller, *Un Allemand à Paris*, p. 164. There could have been among them, including Jünger, no illusion about the fate of Jews in Eastern Europe, concludes Meyer, *Täter im Verhör. Die "Endlösung der Judenfrage" in Frankreich 1940–1944* (Darmstadt, 2005), pp. 282–83.

9. Jünger, "Das Erste Pariser Tagebuch," 16 March 1942, *SW* 2: p. 321.

10. Jünger, "Das Zweite Pariser Tagebuch," 19–21 February 1943, *SW* 3: pp. 11–12.

11. Ibid., 28 February 1943, *SW* 3: pp. 14–15.

12. Ibid., 3–6 March 1943, *SW* 3: pp. 16–18.

13. Ibid., 10, 31 March, 1 April 1943, *SW* 3: pp. 19, 32–33.

14. Ibid., 4 April 1943, *SW* 3: pp. 34–35.

15. Ibid., 16 April 1943, *SW* 3: pp. 41–42. For Jünger, acquaintance with collaborators did not necessarily imply affection for them. On his aversion to Céline, for example, see Venner, *Histoire de la Collaboration*, pp. 213–14; Jackson, *France: The Dark Years*, p. 204; and Albrecht Betz, "Céline entre le IIIe Reich et la France occupée," in Betz and Martens (eds.), *Les intellectuels et l'Occupation*, pp. 90–105.

16. Jünger, "Das Zweite Pariser Tagebuch," 20 April, 3 May 1943, *SW* 3: pp. 48–49, 60.

17. Ibid., 4, 11 May 1943, *SW* 3: pp. 60–61, 69.

18. Ibid., 25 June 1943, *SW* 3: pp. 86–87.

19. Ibid., 10, 18 July 1943, *SW* 3: pp. 96, 103–105.

20. Ibid., 13 July 1943, *SW* 3: p. 100.

21. Ibid., 4, 28 July 1943, *SW* 3: pp. 91–92, 111.

22. Ibid., 29 July, 4, 7, 10 August 1943, *SW* 3: pp. 112, 115, 118–19.

23. Ibid., 21, 27–28, 30 August, 5–6 September 1943, *SW* 3: pp. 126, 133–35, 138, 142–45.

24. Ibid., 16 August 1943, *SW* 3: p. 125.

25. Ibid., 15 September 1943, *SW* 3: pp. 153–55.

26. Ibid.

27. Ibid., 28, 30 October, 8, 13 November 1943, *SW* 3: pp. 183–85, 187, 189.

28. Ibid., 27 November 1943, *SW* 3: pp. 194–95.

29. Ibid., 31 December 1943, *SW* 3: pp. 205–206.

Chapter 7

1. Jünger, "Das Zweite Pariser Tagebuch," 2, 11 January 1944, *SW* 3: pp. 207–11.

2. Ibid., 22 January 1944, *SW* 3: pp. 217–18.

3. Ibid., 16 October 1943, *SW* 3: pp. 173–76. Jünger had been previously sounded out concerning a possible resistance against Hitler by Fritz von der Schulenburg, who was sent by the band of conspirators in Berlin to Paris in the summer of 1943. Their

talks went nowhere. After a second encounter in early October, Schulenburg gave up on Jünger and had no further contact with him. See Wilhelm von Schramm, *Aufstand der Generale. Der 20. Juli in Paris* (2nd ed.; Munich, l964), pp. 11–12; and Kiesel, *Ernst Jünger,* pp. 516–17.

4. Jünger, "Das Zweite Pariser Tagebuch," 29 February, 2–3 March 1944, *SW* 3: pp. 227–31. Jünger's spouse remarked that the chilling episode in Berlin deepened his "melancholy temperament." Gretha Jünger to Benno Ziegler, 12 March 1944, Sammlung des Coudres, DLA Marbach.

5. Jünger, "Das Zweite Pariser Tagebuch," 7 March 1944, *SW* 3: pp. 233–34.

6. Ibid., 27 March 1944, *SW* 3: pp. 240–43. See Gerd R. Ueberschär, "Cäsar von Hofacker und der deutsche Widerstand gegen Hitler in Paris," in Stefan Martens and Maurice Vaïsse (eds.), *Frankreich und Deutschland im Krieg (November 1942–Herbst 1944). Okkupation, Kollaboration, Résistance* (Bonn, 2000), pp. 621–31.

7. Jünger, "Das Zweite Pariser Tagebuch," 27 March 1944, *SW* 3: pp. 240–43.

8. Ibid., 29 March 1944, *SW* 3: pp. 243–44. See Bücheler, *Carl-Heinrich von Stülpnagel,* 284–321.

9. Jünger, "Das Zweite Pariser Tagebuch," 2 April 1944, *SW* 3: pp. 245.

10. Ibid., 21–22 April 1944, *SW* 3: pp. 253.

11. Ibid., 22, 29–30 April 1944, *SW* 3: pp. 253–56.

12. Ibid., 8 May 1944, *SW* 3: pp. 261.

13. Ibid., 13 May 1944, *SW* 3: pp. 263–64. At her Thursday-evening salon, Florence Gould remarked that once the Americans landed on the continent, the Occupation of Paris would be ended within a month. This statement was seconded "without the slightest reserve" by Jünger and his friend Gerhard Heller. Quoted by Michel Jarrety, *Paul Valéry* (Paris, 2008), p. 1153.

14. Jünger, "Das Zweite Pariser Tagebuch," 27 May 1944, *SW* 3: p. 271. However this scene may have been one of Jünger's literary inventions, suggests Kiesel, *Ernst Jünger,* pp. 518–20. Jünger is defended against charges of "aestheticism" by Horst Mühleisen, *Ernst Jünger über den Dächern von Paris. Die Burgunderszene, Dichtung und Wahrheit* (Warmbroon, 2009), pp. 6–9.

15. Jünger, "Das Zweite Pariser Tagebuch," 31 May 1944, *SW* 3: pp. 273–74. "One cannot say that [Stülpnagel] was the driving wedge of the resistance forces, but perhaps this humane man was actually their soul," asserts Schramm, *Aufstand der Generale,* p. 24. The first part of this sentence is more convincing than the second.

16. Jünger to Ziegler, 27 June 1944, Sammlung des Coudres, DLA Marbach.

17. Jünger, "Das Zweite Pariser Tagebuch," 6–8, 17 June 1945, *SW* 3: pp. 277–80

18. Ibid. In 1938 Trott had visited Jünger in Überlingen, and he took the initiative to seek him out in Paris. Heinrich von Trott zu Solz to Jünger, 3 November 1940, 17 July 1943, A-Jünger, DLA Marbach.

19. Jünger, "Das Zweite Pariser Tagebuch," 24 June, 1 July 1944, *SW* 3: pp. 281–83.

20. Ibid., 13 July 1944, *SW* 3: p. 285.

21. Ibid., 16 July 1944, *SW* 3: p. 287.

22. Schramm, *Aufstand der Generale,* p. 68.

23. Ibid., pp. 116–34.

24. Jünger, "Das Zweite Pariser Tagebuch," 21 July 1944, *SW* 3: pp. 288–89.

25. Quoted by Schramm, *Aufstand der Generale,* p. 144.

26. Jünger, "Das Zweite Pariser Tagebuch," 22 July 1944, *SW* 3: pp. 289–90. See Bücheler, *Carl-Heinrich von Stülpnagel*, pp. 321–38; and Mitchell, *Nazi Paris*, pp. 139–40.
27. Schwilk, *Ernst Jünger*, p. 403.
28. Jünger, "Das Zweite Pariser Tagebuch," 5 August 1944, *SW* 3: p. 293.
29. Ibid., 8 August 1944, *SW* 3: p. 293.
30. Jünger, "Kirchhorster Blätter," 14–17 August, 1 September 1944, *SW* 3: pp. 297, 303.

Chapter 8

1. Gerhard Loose, *Ernst Jünger: Gestalt und Werk* (Frankfurt a. M., 1957), p. 32. "As was already the case during the First World War, the text that we read does not at all constitute a spontaneous reaction to the lived experience," comments Hervier (ed.), *Ernst Jünger*, 2: p. 1129. See Böhme, *Fassungen bei Ernst Jünger*, pp. 104–30; and Dempewolf, *Blut und Tinte*, pp. 78–92.
2. See Krömer, "Die Handschriften von Ernst Jüngers Pariser Tagebüchern," pp. 337–51.
3. Neaman, *A Dubious Past*, p. 143. "But here there may have been an error about the person" [of Florence's lover], cautions Hervier (ed.), *Ernst Jünger*, 2: p. 1298. For further details in this regard about her and Sophie Ravoux, see the Postscript.
4. Jünger to Armin Mohler, 9 August 1947, A-Jünger, DLA Marbach.
5. Jünger, "Das Erste Pariser Tagebuch," 18 August 1942, *SW* 2: p. 367. See Neaman, *A Dubious Past*, pp. 144–45; and Burrin, *La France à l'heure allemande*, p. 204.
6. See the most caustic and uncompromising criticism of Jünger by Peter de Mendelssohn, "Gegenstrahlungen," *Der Monat* 14 (1949): pp. 149–74.
7. See Bernd Hüppauf, "Whereof Ernst Jünger cannot speak, thereof he can also not be silent," in Andrew Bonnell et al. (eds.), *Power, Conscience, and Opposition* (New York, Washington D.C., and Bern, 1996), pp. 345–63.
8. The polemics continue to this day, as in the sharp counterattack by Hans-Ulrich Wehler, "Die fundamentale Untat: Eine Replik auf Ernst Nolte," *Frankfurter Allgemeine Zeitung*, 1 October 2008.
9. See Krömer, "Die Handschriften von Ernst Jüngers Tagebüchern," pp. 347–49.
10. The army's role is seen more positively in older works like Eberhard Jäckel, *Frankreich in Hitlers Europa. Die deutsche Frankreichpolitik im Zweiten Weltkrieg* (Stuttgart, 1966); and Umbreit, *Der Militärbefehlshaber in Frankreich*. A more critical tone is evident in Meyer, *Die deutsche Besatzung in Frankreich*; and Regina Delacor (ed.), *Attentate und Repressionen. Ausgewählte Dokumente zur zyklischen Eskalation des NS-Terrors im besetzten Frankreich 1941/42* (Stuttgart, 2000). This subject is treated throughout by Mitchell, *Nazi Paris*, passim.
11. See Mohler, *Die konservative Revolution in Deutschland 1918–1932*, 2nd ed. (Darmstadt, 1972), pp. 94–97; and Kiesel, "Zwischen Kritik und Affirmation: Ernst Jüngers Auseinandersetzung mit dem Nationalsozialismus," in Günther Rüther (ed.), *Literatur in der Diktatur. Schreiben im Nationalsozialismus und DDR-Sozialismus* (Paderborn, 1997), pp. 163–72.
12. Bullock, *The Violent Eye*, p. 129.

13. Quoted by Hervier, *Entretiens avec Ernst Jünger*, pp. 103–104. Through all of Jünger's revisions of texts and altered versions of his journals, "the clearly positive interpretation of war remained," concludes Dempewolf, *Blut und Tinte*, p. 272.

Chapter 9

1. Jünger, "Kirchhorster Blätter," 17, 23 August, 7, 9 September, 2 October 1944, *SW* 3: pp. 298, 300, 304–305, 308.
2. Ibid., 6, 11–12, 20 October 1944, *SW* 3: pp. 309–10, 312–13.
3. Ibid., 1 November 1944, 12–14 January, 15 March 1945, *SW* 3: pp. 315, 360, 382.
4. Ibid., 5, 15, 26–28 November, 13 December 1944, 6 February 1945, *SW* 3: pp. 320, 326, 331–32, 341, 367.
5. Ibid., 14, 16, 18 December 1944, *SW* 3: pp. 342, 345–46.
6. Ibid., 15, 29 December 1944, *SW* 3: pp. 343–44, 349–50.
7. Ibid., 9, 23 January, 14 February, 9 March 1945, *SW* 3: pp. 358, 362, 370–71, 380.
8. Ibid., 20 March 1945, *SW* 3: pp. 387.
9. Ibid., 28 March 1945, *SW* 3: pp. 389–90.
10. Ibid., 29 March 1945, *SW* 3: pp. 390.
11. Ibid., 1, 5–6, 10–11 April 1945, *SW* 3: pp. 391, 395–96, 398–401.
12. Jünger, "Die Hütte im Weinberg," 29 April, 1 May 1945, *SW* 3: pp. 420–21.
13. Ibid., 7 May 1945, *SW* 3: pp. 432–33.
14. Ibid., 8, 10 May 1945, *SW* 3: pp. 434, 440–41.
15. Ibid., 14 April, 12 May 1945, *SW* 3: pp. 412, 446–49. Full disclosure: the author was raised in Kentucky and resents that remark!
16. Ibid., 23 May 1945, *SW* 3: pp. 454–55. See Schwilk, *Ernst Jünger*, pp. 434–35.
17. Jünger, "Die Hütte im Weinberg," 23 May, 2 June 1945, *SW* 3: pp. 453–54, 463.
18. Ibid., 15 June 1945, *SW* 3: pp. 475–76.
19. Ibid., 26 June, 29 July 1945, *SW* 3: pp. 481–83, 497.
20. Ibid., 21 July, 22 August 1945, *SW* 3: pp. 493, 511–15.
21. Ibid., 24 August, 24 September 1945, *SW* 3: pp. 515–19, 548–54. On the function of the MBF, Jünger later commented that it was "less self-important than the Parisians imagined. It was a bureaucratic post that brought much trouble and little reward." Jünger, *Jahre der Okkupation* (Stuttgart, 1958), p. 176.
22. Jünger, "Die Hütte im Weinberg," 28 March–2 April 1946, *SW* 3: pp. 605–17.
23. Ibid., 15 September 1945, 2 April 1946, *SW* 3: pp. 540, 617. See Mitchell, *Nazi Paris*, pp. 151–55.
24. Schwilk, *Ernst Jünger*, pp. 439–41.
25. Jünger, *Heliopolis. Rückblicke auf eine Stadt* (Tübingen, 1949). "In *Heliopolis* Jünger worked through the sum of the experiences that he had collected in Paris," writes Schwilk, *Ernst Jünger. Leben und Werk*, p. 308. He received a harsh critique from his nemesis Peter de Mendelssohn: "In my opinion it is such a complete and total confusion of artistic taste that I cannot at all approach the conception (*Gedankengebäude*)." Mendelssohn to Jünger, 20 December 1949, A-Jünger, DLA Marbach. See Wolfgang Kaempfer, *Ernst Jünger* (Stuttgart, 1981), pp. 129–46; Kiesel, *Ernst Jünger*, pp. 558–73; and Rolf Hayer, "'Über dieses Buch hinaus gibt es für Jünger keine Entwicklung mehr...'—Ernst Jüngers *Heliopolis* im Spiegel der Literaturkritik," in Zarska et al. (eds.), *Ernst Jünger—eine Bilanz*, pp. 498–509.

26. Jünger is cited by Noack, *Ernst Jünger,* pp. 239. See Schwilk, *Ernst Jünger,* pp. 442, 461–62, 465–66; and Kiesel, *Ernst Jünger,* pp. 584–86. For details of Jünger's correspondence with Sophie Ravoux after the war, see the Postscript.

27. See Schwilk, *Ernst Jünger,* pp. 447–48; and Kiesel, *Ernst Jünger,* pp. 588–98.

Chapter 10

1. Bargatzky, *Hotel Majestic,* pp. 54–55.

2. Jünger to Breitbach, 17 November 1952, A-Jünger, DLA Marbach. Heinrich von Stülpnagel was described as "the most perfect nobleman I have ever met" by Bargatzky, *Hotel Majestic,* pp. 54–55. The same sentiment was expressed in a letter from Ernst Schaer to Jünger, 31 October 1949, A-Jünger, DLA Marbach.

3. Jünger to Bargatzky, 2 September 1983, A-Jünger, DLA Marbach. Bargatzky, *Hotel Majestic,* pp. 80–82.

4. Speidel to Jünger, 10 December 1947, 17 January 1948, 11 February 1952, 30 January 1956, A-Jünger, DLA Marbach. Speidel, *Aus unserer Zeit,* pp. 109–12.

5. Grüninger to Jünger, 8 December 1941, 20, 28 March 1942, 10 January 1945, A-Jünger, DLA Marbach.

6. Podewils to Jünger, 8 April 1942 and passim, ibid.

7. Heller to Jünger, 22 January 1943, ibid.

8. Heller to Jünger, 3 December 1943, 25 February 1946, ibid. Jünger to Heller, 28 April 1967, ibid. Heller, *Un Allemand à Paris,* pp. 161–63, 169. See Alan Riding, *And The Show Went On: Cultural Life in Nazi-Occupied Paris* (New York, 2010), pp. 255–68.

9. Nebel to Jünger, [spring of] 1942, A-Jünger, DLA Marbach.

10. Nebel to Jünger, 1 December 1945, ibid. Nebel, *Ernst Jünger. Abenteuer des Geistes* (Wuppertal, 1949), pp. 125–35, 282–84.

11. Jünger to Nebel, 12 February, 7 April 1949, A-Jünger, DLA Marbach. The same evaluation of England and France, precisely at a time when he was moving from the English to the French zone, was stated by Jünger to Heidegger, 11 June 1949, ibid.

12. Jünger to Nebel, 6 September 1967, ibid.

13. Breitbach to Jünger, 1 June 1938, ibid.

14. Breitbach to Jünger, 17 October, 19 November 1951, ibid.

15. Heidegger to Jünger, 1 January 1956, ibid.

16. Jünger to Heidegger, 2 February 1959, ibid. Heidegger to Jünger, 22 November 1960, ibid.

17. The Marbach archive contains sixteen letters from Jünger to Heidegger between 1966 and 1974. See Kaempfer, *Ernst Jünger,* pp. 119–28.

18. Heidegger, *Gesamtausgabe,* 90 vols.; (Frankfurt a. M., 1978–2004), 90: pp. 236–39.

19. Ibid., 259, 263–66, 277. For further detail, see Daniel Morat, *Von der Tat zur Gelassenheit. Konservatives Denken bei Martin Heidegger, Ernst Jünger und Friedrich Georg Jünger* (Göttingen, 2007).

20. Fischer to Jünger, 8 May 1933, A-Jünger, DLA Marbach.

21. Nebel to Jünger, 2 August 1939, ibid. One person who often saw Schmitt and Jünger together in the prewar years was Ernst Niekisch, *Erinnerungen eines deutschen Revolutionärs,* 2 vols. (Cologne, 1974), 1: pp. 187–92. See Noack, *Ernst Jünger,* pp. 259–70.

22. Schmitt to Jünger, 29 September 1940, 4 July, 16 August, 5 October 1941, A-Jünger, DLA Marbach. Jünger to Schmitt, 17 December 1944, 20 December 1957, 26 June 1973, ibid..

23. Several relevant editions of portions of Jünger's correspondence have appeared in print. Among them: Helmuth Kiesel (ed.), *Ernst Jünger-Carl Schmitt Briefwechsel 1930-1983* (Stuttgart, 1999); and Ulrich Fröschle and Michael Neumann (eds.), *Ernst Jünger-Gerhard Nebel Briefwechsel 1938-1974* (Stuttgart, 2003). As his endnotes testify, the author who has made the most extensive use of correspondence housed in the Marbach archive is Schwilk, *Ernst Jünger*, pp. 575-612.

24. Jünger to Jouhandeau, 14 September 1951, A-Jünger, DLA Marbach.

25. Jünger to Gracq, 27 November 1952, ibid.

26. Montherlant to Jünger, 21 August 1942, ibid.

27. Benoist-Méchin to Jünger, 8 October 1941, ibid. See David Boal, *Journaux intimes sous l'occupation* (Paris, 1993), pp. 41-55.

28. Drieu la Rochelle to Jünger, 5 February, 1 March 1942, A-Jünger, DLA Marbach. No mention is made of Jünger in Drieu la Rochelle, *Journal 1939-1945* (Paris, 1992). For comparison of the two, see Hervier, *Deux individus contre l'histoire. Pierre Drieu La Rochelle, Ernst Jünger* (Poitiers, 1978).

29. Cocteau to Jünger, [nd] December 1941, A-Jünger, DLA Marbach.

30. On the relations between Jünger and Léautaud, among other French intellectuals, see Boal, *Journaux intimes sous l'occupation,* pp. 75-138. Léautaud, "who, famous for his love of cats and contempt for his fellow French (especially Jews), had no trouble with the German presence" in Paris, comments Nevin, *Ernst Jünger and Germany,* p. 182.

31. Jünger to Breitbach, 17 November 1952, A-Jünger, DLA Marbach. Jünger to Céline, 11 September 1951, ibid. Jünger habitually wrote Céline's name without an accent mark.

32. Heller to Jünger, 25 February 1946, 4 February 1949, ibid. Paulhan to Jünger, 2 March, 28 May 1951, ibid.

33. Fabre-Luce to Jünger, 23 December 1941, 29 June 1942, ibid.

34. Fabre-Luce to Jünger, 23 September 1954, 20 January 1955, 1 December 1967, ibid.

35. *Carte pneumatique,* addressed to the Hotel Raphael, from Jouhandeau to Jünger, [nd] August 1943, ibid.

36. Heller to Jünger, 25 February 1946, 4 February 1949, 28 March 1952, ibid. Jünger to Jouhandeau, 11 September 1951, ibid. Jouhandeau to Jünger, 13, 19 September 1951, ibid. Jünger explained that he preferred to send typed letters in German "because I am more secure [and] because it is more legible—two faults, I hope, that cancel each other out." Jünger to Gracq, 27 November 1952, ibid.

37. Jünger to Jouhandeau, 15 January 1958, ibid. Jünger later stated in an interview: "Jouhandeau pleases me particularly by his style. It's an exception in our time." Quoted by Hervier, *Entretiens avec Ernst Jünger,* p. 126. See Thierry Sete, *La perception de la France dans l'oeuvre d'Ernst Jünger* (Metz, 1997), pp. 14-15.

38. Jouhandeau, "Reconnaissance à Ernst Jünger," *Antaios* 6 (1965): pp. 438-40.

39. Jouhandeau to Jünger, 26 November 1967, A-Jünger, DLA Marbach. Jünger to Jouhandeau, 3 March 1970, 27 May 1973, ibid.

Postscript

1. Banine to Jünger, 12 and 13 October 1942, A-Jünger, DLA Marbach. See Kiesel, *Ernst Jünger*, pp. 509, 543–44.
2. Banine to Jünger, 28 February 1946, A-Jünger, DLA Marbach. Jünger to Banine, 12 May 1946, ibid.
3. Apparently this appellation was derived from a plant with white flowers, *gypsophile*, which Jünger had sent to Sophie.
4. Banine to Jünger, 22 May, 12 July, 6 September, 5 October 1946, A-Jünger, DLA Marbach. Jünger to Banine, 10 September, 5 October 1947, ibid.
5. Banine to Jünger, 13 and 26 November 1946, 20 April 1947, ibid.
6. Banine to Jünger, 10 July, 16 September, 12 October 1947, ibid.
7. Banine to Jünger, 10 December 1947, ibid.
8. Banine, *Rencontres avec Ernst Jünger* (Paris, 1951), pp. 9–64.
9. Banine to Jünger, 23 July, 7 August, 28 September 1950, A-Jünger, DLA Marbach.
10. Banine to Jünger, 2 October 1950, ibid.
11. Banine to Jünger, 2 April 1952, ibid.
12. Banine to Jünger, 12 May, 27 June 1952, ibid. See Kiesel, *Ernst Jünger*, p. 509.
13. Banine, *Portrait d'Ernst Jünger. Lettres, Textes et Rencontres* (Paris, 1971), pp. 167, 236.
14. "La mort de la grande amie d'Ernst Jünger," *Figaro*, 29 October 1992.
15. Alexandra Felts, "Eine Amerikanerin in Paris," *Madame* 10 (1990): pp. 102–104, 216. Further details of her life were presented in an obituary, "Florence Gould (1895–1983)," *Schweizerische Handelszeitung*, 2 May 1983.
16. Dominique Aury, "Tout le monde l'appelait Florence," *Le Monde*, 3 March 1983. "Le Salon de Florence Gould," ibid., 16 March 1983.
17. See Wimbauer, *Personenregister*, p. 118.
18. Heller to Jünger, 3 December 1943, A-Jünger, DLA Marbach. Heller, *Un Allemand à Paris*, p. 163.
19. "Message téléphonique pour Monsieur le Capitaine Jünger," 12 September 1943, A-Jünger, DLA Marbach. See Riding, *And The Show Went On*, pp. 255–68.
20. Sophie Ravoux to Jünger, 31 October 1985, A-Jünger, DLA Marbach.
21. See Kiesel, *Ernst Jünger*, pp. 505–509.
22. For example, see the entries about strolls with "Charmille" through the Rue du Faubourg St.-Honoré and the park of Vincennes in Jünger, "Das Erste Pariser Tagebuch," 18 and 23 September 1942, SW 2: pp. 381–82.
23. Two letters from Sophie Ravoux to Jünger, 16 December 1942, A-Jünger, DLA Marbach.
24. Valentiner to Jünger, 6 February 1943, ibid.
25. Sophie Ravoux to Jünger, 16 August 1944, ibid.
26. Sophie Ravoux to Jünger, 5 August, 14 September 1945, ibid.
27. Jünger to Sophie Ravoux, 10 January 1946, ibid.
28. Sophie Ravoux to Jünger, 3 March [1948], ibid. Because 3 March 1946 was a Sunday and 3 March 1947 a Monday, only 3 March 1948, a Wednesday, fits all the known facts.

29. Gretha Jünger to Sophie Ravoux, 9 September 1948, ibid. In a veiled reference, Jünger's wife referred to this circumstance in a later memoir: "On the legitimate mate and the beloved: between the reigning woman (*Herrscherin*) and the favorite a struggle for power can only originate from the latter. That proves that she has more to fear from a defeat." Gretha von Jeinsen, *Die Palette. Tagebuchblätter und Briefe* (Hamburg, 1949), pp. 62–63.

30. Sophie Ravoux to Jünger, 5 December 1957, A-Jünger, DLA Marbach.

31. Sophie Ravoux to Jünger, 3 February, 27 March 1958, ibid.

32. Sophie Ravoux to Jünger, 4 January 1959, 28 June 1960, ibid.

33. Sophie Ravoux to Jünger, 22 January, 18 May, 19 June, 5 and 18 July, 31 August, 28 October, 4 and 15 December 1961, ibid.

34. Sophie Ravoux to Jünger, 9 February 1962, ibid.

35. Sophie Ravoux to Jünger, 16 February 1962, ibid.

36. Jünger to Sophie Ravoux, 20 March 1972, ibid. Sophie Ravoux to Jünger, 20 and 31 August, 9 September 1972, ibid. See Schwilk, *Ernst Jünger,* p. 537.

37. Sophie Ravoux to Jünger, 10 August 1984, A-Jünger, DLA Marbach.

Conclusion

1. Bullock, *The Violent Eye*, pp. 11–17. For a similar view, see Lukács, *Die Zerstörung der Vernunft*, pp. 462–66; Herf, *Reactionary Modernism*, pp. 81–96; and Dupeux, "Der 'Neue Nationalismus' Ernst Jüngers," in Koslowski (ed.), *Die grossen Jagden des Mythos*, pp. 15–40.

2. For instance, see Rainer Gruenter, "Formen des Dandysmus. Eine problemgeschichtliche Studie über Ernst Jünger," *Euphorion* 46 (1952): pp. 170–202; Bohrer, *Die Ästhetik des Schreckens*, pp. 31–41; Kaempfer, *Ernst Jünger*, pp. 157–64; Brandes, *Der "Neue Stil" in Ernst Jüngers"Strahlungen,"* pp. 215–64; and Jörg Sader, *"Im Bauch des Leviathan." Tagebuch und Maskerade. Anmerkungen zu Ernst Jüngers "Strahlungen" (1939–1948)* (Würzburg, 1996).

Selected Bibliography

Apart from housing Ernst Jünger's manuscripts and correspondence, the Deutsches Literaturarchiv in Marbach contains the most complete and current bibliography concerning his life and works. Otherwise, the starting point for a survey of his writings is Horst Mühleisen (ed.), *Bibliographie der Werke Ernst Jüngers* (Stuttgart, 1996). A listing of commentaries on them has been gathered by Nicolai Riedel (ed.), *Ernst Jünger-Bibliographie: wissenschaftliche und essayistische Beiträge zu seinem Werk (1928–2002)* (Stuttgart and Weimar, 2003). Very useful are the thirty pages of bibliographical overview astutely presented by Helmuth Kiesel in his biography of Jünger, which is listed among the selected secondary readings below.

Azéma, Jean-Pierre, and François Bédarida (eds.). *La France des années noires*. 2 vols. Paris, 1993.
Barnouw, Dagmar. *Weimar Intellectuals and the Threat of Modernity*. Bloomington and Indianapolis, 1988.
Berghahn, Volker R. *Der Stahlhelm. Bund der Frontsoldaten 1918–1935*. Düsseldorf, 1966.
Betz, Albrecht, and Stefan Martens (eds.). *Les intellectuels et l'Occupation. Collaborer, partir, résister*. Paris, 2004.
Boal, David. *Journaux intimes sous l'occupation*. Paris, 1993.
Böhme, Ulrich. *Fassungen bei Ernst Jünger*. Meisenheim am Glan, 1972.
Bohrer, Karl-Heinz. *Die Ästhetik des Schreckens. Die pessimistische Romantik und Ernst Jüngers Frühwerk*. Munich and Vienna, 1978.
Brandes, Wolfgang. *Der "Neue Stil" in Ernst Jüngers "Strahlungen." Genese, Funktion und Realitätsproduktion des literarischen Ich in seinen Tagebüchern*. Bonn, 1990.
Bücheler, Heinrich. *Carl-Heinrich von Stülpnagel. Soldat—Philosoph—Verschwörer*. Berlin and Frankfurt a. M., 1989.
Buisson, Patrick. *1940–1945 Années érotiques. Vichy ou les infortunes de la vertu*. Paris, 2008.

Bullock, Marcus Paul. *The Violent Eye: Ernst Jünger's Visions and Revisions on the European Right.* Detroit, 1992.
Burrin, Philippe. *La France à l'heure allemande 1940-1944.* Paris, 1995.
Dempewolf, Eva. *Blut und Tinte. Eine Interpretation der verschiedenen Fassungen von Ernst Jüngers Kriegstagebüchern vor dem politischen Hintergrund der Jahre 1920 bis 1981.* Würzburg, 1992.
Herbert, Ulrich. *Best. Biographische Studien über Radikalismus, Weltanschauung und Vernunft, 1903-1989.* Bonn, 1996.
Herf, Jeffrey. *Reactionary Modernism. Technology, Culture, and Politics in Weimar and the Third Reich.* Cambridge, 1984.
Hervier, Julien. *Deux individus contre l'histoire: Pierre Drieu La Rochelle, Ernst Jünger.* Poitiers, 1978.
Jackson, Julian. *France: The Dark Years 1940-1944.* Oxford, 2001.
Jäckel, Eberhard. *Frankreich in Hitlers Europa. Die deutsche Frankreichpolitik im Zweiten Weltkrieg.* Stuttgart, 1966.
Kaempfer, Wolfgang. *Ernst Jünger.* Stuttgart, 1981.
Kiesel, Helmuth. *Ernst Jünger. Die Biographie.* Munich, 2007.
King, John. *"Wann hat dieser Scheisskrieg ein Ende?" Writing and Rewriting the First World War.* Schnellroda, 2003.
Klemperer, Klemens von. *Germany's New Conservatism: Its History and Dilemma in the Twentieth Century.* Princeton, 1957.
Koslowski, Peter (ed.). *Die grossen Jagden des Mythos. Ernst Jünger in Frankreich.* Munich, 1996.
Krömer, Felix. "Offizier und Tagebuchautor im besetzten Paris. Die Darstellung des NS-Regimes in Ernst Jüngers Journalen 1941-1944." Unpublished *Magisterarbeit* at the Humboldt University. Berlin, 2004.
Loose, Gerhard. *Ernst Jünger: Gestalt und Werk.* Frankfurt a. M., 1957.
Lukács, Georg. *Die Zerstörung der Vernunft.* Neuwied am Rhein and Berlin, 1962.
Martens, Stefan, and Maurice Vaïsse (eds.). *Frankreich und Deutschland im Krieg (November 1942-Herbst 1944). Okkupation, Kollaboration, Résistance.* Bonn, 2000.
Martus, Steffen. *Ernst Jünger.* Stuttgart and Weimar, 2001.
Mazower, Mark. *Hitler's Empire: How the Nazis Ruled Europe.* New York, 2008.
Mendelssohn, Peter de. *Der Geist in der Despotie: Versuche über die moralischen Möglichkeiten des Intellektuellen in der totalitären Gesellschaft.* Berlin, 1953.
Meyer, Ahlrich. *Die deutsche Besatzung in Frankreich 1940-1944. Widerstandsbekämpfung und Judenverfolgung.* Darmstadt, 2000.
_____. *Täter im Verhör. Die "Endlösung der Judenfrage" in Frankreich 1940-1944.* Darmstadt, 2005.
Meyer, Martin. *Ernst Jünger.* Munich and Vienna, 1990.
Mitchell, Allan. *Nazi Paris: The History of an Occupation, 1940-1944.* New York and Oxford, 2008.
Mohler, Armin. *Die konservative Revolution in Deutschland 1918-1932.* 2nd ed. Darmstadt, 1972.
Morat, Daniel. *Von der Tat zur Gelassenheit. Konservatives Denken bei Martin Heidegger, Ernst Jünger und Friedrich Georg Jünger.* Göttingen, 2007.
Mühleisen, Horst. *Ernst Jünger in Berlin, 1927-1933.* Frankfurt an der Oder, 1998.

———. *Ernst Jünger über den Dächern von Paris. Die Burgunderszene, Dichtung und Wahrheit*. Warmbroon, 2009.
Müller, Hans-Harald. *Der Krieg und die Schriftsteller. Der Kriegsroman der Weimarer Republik*. Stuttgart, 1986.
Müller, Hans-Harald, and Harro Segeberg (eds.). *Ernst Jünger im 20. Jahrhundert*. Munich, 1995.
Neaman, Elliot Y. *A Dubious Past: Ernst Jünger and the Politics of Literature after Nazism*. Berkeley, Los Angeles, and London, 1999.
Nevin, Thomas. *Ernst Jünger and Germany: Into the Abyss, 1914–1945*. Durham, North Carolina, 1996.
Noack, Paul. *Ernst Jünger: eine Biographie*. Berlin, 1998.
Pelletier, Nicole, et al. (eds.). *L'Allemagne et la crise de la raison*. Bordeaux, 2001.
Riding, Alan. *And The Show Went On: Cultural Life in Nazi-Occupied Paris*. New York, 2010.
Rüther, Günther (ed.). *Literatur in der Diktatur. Schreiben im Nationalsozialismus und DDR-Sozialismus*. Paderborn, 1997.
Ryback, Timothy W. *Hitler's Private Library: The Books that Shaped His Life*. New York, 2009.
Sader, Jörg. *"Im Bauch des Leviathan." Tagebuch und Maskerade. Anmerkungen zu Ernst Jüngers "Strahlungen" (1939–1948)*. Würzburg, 1996.
Scherer, Helmut (ed.). *Dichter und ihre Nation*. Frankfurt a. M., 1993.
Schramm, Wilhelm von. *Aufstand der Generale: Der 20. Juli in Paris*. 2nd ed. Munich, 1964.
Schwarz, Hans-Peter. *Der konservative Anarchist. Politik und Zeitkritik Ernst Jüngers*. Freiburg im Breisgau, 1962.
Schwilk, Heimo. *Ernst Jünger. Ein Jahrhundertleben*. Munich and Zurich, 2007.
———. *Ernst Jünger. Leben und Werk in Bildern und Texten*. Stuttgart, 1988.
Sete, Thierry. *La perception de la France dans l'oeuvre d'Ernst Jünger*. Metz, 1997.
Sontheimer, Kurt. *Antidemokratisches Denken in der Weimarer Republik. Die politischen Ideen des deutschen Nationalismus zwischen 1918 und 1933*. Munich, 1962.
Traureck, Margot. *Friedrich Sieburg in Frankreich. Seine literarisch-publizistischen Stellungnahmen zwischen den Weltkriegen in Vergleich mit Positionen Ernst Jüngers*. Heidelberg, 1987.
Umbreit, Hans. *Der Militärbefehlshaber in Frankreich 1940–1944*. Boppard, 1968.
Venner, Dominique. *Histoire de la Collaboration*. Paris, 2000.
Vinen, Richard. *The Unfree French. Life under the Occupation*. New Haven and London, 2006.
Volmert, Johannes. *Ernst Jünger: "In Stahlgewittern."* Munich, 1985.
Wimbauer, Tobias. *Personenregister der Tagebücher Ernst Jüngers*. 2nd ed. Schnellroda, 2003.
Zarska, Natalia, Gerald Diesner, and Wojciech Kunicki (eds.). *Ernst Jünger—eine Bilanz*. Leipzig, 2010.

Name Index

Abetz, Otto, 23, 53
Alain-Fournier, Henri, 47
Arendt, Hannah, 64
Arletty, 23
Aury, Dominique, 83

Balzac, Honoré de, 64
Banine (Umm-El-Banine Assadoulaeff), 79–82, 84, 87
Bargatzky, Walter, 69, 98n41
Barnouw, Dagmar, 6
Barrès, Maurice, 5
Baudelaire, Charles, 5, 10, 28
Benn, Gottfried, 5
Benoist-Méchin, Jacques, 43, 46, 61, 75
Best, Werner, 18, 21–22, 24, 69, 96n15
Bloy, Léon, 14, 64
Boëthius, 15
Bohrer, Karl-Heinz, 4
Bonnard, Abel, 43, 76
Bosch, Heronimus, 16, 31
Boudot-Lamotte, Madame, 25
Boulanger, Georges, 63
Braque, Georges, 98n35
Breitbach, Josef, 72
Breker, Arno, 25
Brinon, Fernand de, 23
Brueghel, Pieter, 16
Bullock, Marcus Paul, 5
Burckhardt, Jacob, 16

Casanova, Giacomo, 15, 57

Céline, Louis-Ferdinand, 43, 76–77, 106n31
Cherubini, Maria Luigi Carlo, 28
Choltitz, Dietrich von, 61, 64
Chopin, Frédéric François, 28
Churchill, Winston, 64
Clausewitz, Karl von, 38, 65
Cocteau, Jean, 24–27, 42–43, 75, 77, 89
Conan Doyle, Arthur, 18
Cooper, James Fenimore, 8
Corday, Charlotte, 25
Coudres, Hans Peter des, 95n13
Cramer von Laue, Constantin, 45, 62, 69, 74

Déat, Marcel, 43
Dostoyevsky, Fedor, 8, 48
Drieu la Rochelle, Pierre, 24, 27, 61, 75

Eisner, Kurt, 64
Epting, Karl, 69, 71
Erasmus, Desiderius, 14

Fabre-Luce, Alfred, 71, 75–77
Fischer, Hugo, 73
France, Anatole, 15
Franz Ferdinand, Archduke, 25
Frederick the Great, 42
Freud, Sigmund, 30, 45

Gallimard, Gaston, 24–25, 75
Gaulle, Charles de, 36
Gide, André, 14, 48, 72, 76
Giraud, Henri, 36

Giraudoux, Jean, 42–43
Goebbels, Joseph, 40–41, 57
Goerdeler, Carl, 49
Goethe, Johann Wolfgang von, 5, 8
Gogol, Nikolai, 38
Gould, Florence, 27, 42, 57, 61, 69, 71, 76–77, 82–84, 102n13, 103n3
Gould, Frank Jay, 83
Gould, Jay, 83
Gracq, Julien, 74, 76
Green, Julien, 72
Grüninger, Horst, 22, 24, 69
Guinness, Alec, 25
Guitry, Sacha, 23

Hebbel, Friedrich, 15
Hegel, Georg Wilhelm Friedrich, 65
Heidegger, Martin, 69, 72–73
Heller, Gerhard, 71, 76–77, 83, 86, 102n13
Henri IV, 28
Herodotus, 8, 14
Hesiod, 15
Hess, Rudolf, 41
Hielscher, Friedrich, 47, 57
Himmler, Heinrich, 57, 64
Hitler, Adolf, 3, 12, 26, 35–36, 40–46, 48–52, 54, 57–58, 60–65, 67, 90
Hofacker, Cäsar von, 48–50, 52–54, 65
Hoffmann, E. T. A., 5
Hölderlin, Friedrich, 47
Homer, 8
Horton, Morris, 23, 97n12
Huxley, Aldous, 44–45

Jeanne d'Arc, 18, 21
Jouhandeau, Marcel, 71, 74, 77–78, 106n37
Jünger, Ernst Georg (father), 8, 32–33, 38, 43, 45, 47, 61–62, 76, 99n4
Jünger, Ernstel (son), 11–12, 48, 50, 85
Jünger, Friedrich Georg (brother), 43, 67
Jünger, Gretha (first wife, *née* von Jeinsen), 2, 10–12, 18, 24–25, 27, 29, 31, 33–35, 37–38, 42–43, 50, 55, 57, 60, 66–67, 73, 85–88, 90, 92n11, 108n29
Jünger, Karoline (mother), 31
Jünger, Liselotte (second wife, *née* Bäuerle), 82, 88, 98n21

Kafka, Franz, 1, 6
Katte, Martin von, 64, 69

Kiesel, Helmuth, 4–5
Kleist, Ewald von, 36, 38
Klemperer, Klemens von, 6
Kluge, Günther von, 65
Kossmann, Karl-Richard, 29

Labusquière, Jean, 75
Léautaud, Paul, 71, 76, 106n30
Lessing, Gotthold, 8

Malraux, André, 24
Mann, Heinrich, 7
Mann, Thomas, 1, 5–6
Mansfield, Katherine, 47
Marais, Jean, 25, 27
Marat, Jean Paul, 25
Marcel, Gabriel, 74
Martus, Steffen, 4
Marx, Karl, 11, 92n15
May, Karl, 8
Melville, Herman, 15
Mendelssohn, Peter de, 4
Meyer, Martin, 4
Moltke, Helmuth von, 15
Monet, Claude, 53
Montherlant, Henry de, 15, 34, 61, 75
Musil, Robert, 1
Mussolini, Benito, 44, 63

Neaman, Elliot, 5–6, 94n10
Nebel, Gerhard, 71–72, 74
Nevin, Thomas, 6
Niekisch, Ernst, 11, 57
Nietzsche, Friedrich, 8, 10–11, 16, 73
Nolte, Ernst, 58

Oberg, Carl, 53

Paulhan, Jean, 71, 76–77
Paulus, Friedrich, 38
Pepys, Samuel, 48
Pétain, Henri Philippe, 17, 35
Picasso, Pablo, 28
Podewils, Clemens, 21–22, 24, 50, 53, 69

Ravoux, Paul, 24, 80–81, 84–85, 87–88
Ravoux, Sophie, 4, 24–29, 42–43, 47, 54, 57, 60, 66, 71, 79–81, 84–90, 97n19
Rimbaud, Arthur, 5, 10, 38
Rommel, Erwin, 50–52

Roosevelt, Franklin D., 64
Rundstedt, Gerd von, 50, 65

Salomon, Ernst von, 11
Sandemont, Jeanne, 9
Schaer, Ernst, 64, 69
Schaumburg, Ernst, 21
Schiller, Friedrich, 8
Schleier, Rudolf, 23
Schlumberger, Jean, 72, 76
Schmitt, Carl, 24, 31, 35, 37–38, 43, 48, 66, 69, 73–74
Schopenhauer, Arthur, 8, 94n2
Schulenburg, Fritz von der, 101n3
Schwarz, Hans-Peter, 4, 6
Sieburg, Friedrich, 24
Sontheimer, Kurt, 4, 6
Speidel, Hans, 21–24, 26–27, 33, 37, 41–42, 50–52, 61, 69, 76
Spengler, Oswald, 5, 10–11, 14, 32, 73
Stalin, Joseph, 58
Stauffenberg, Claus Schenk von, 49, 53–54, 67
Stauffenberg, Franz Schenk von, 67

Stendhal, 8
Strasser, Otto, 100n2
Stülpnagel, Heinrich von, 26, 28–29, 33–34, 44, 49–54, 59–61, 64–65, 69, 102n15, 105n2
Stülpnagel, Otto von, 26, 33, 59, 65, 69

Tacitus, 8
Tocqueville, Alexis de, 48
Tolkien, J. R. R., 12
Trott zu Solz, Adam von, 52
Trott zu Solz, Heinrich von, 52
Twain, Mark, 8

Ulysses, 9

Valentiner, Claus, 25–27, 29, 37, 71, 85–86
Valéry, Paul, 43
Verlaine, Paul, 61

Wilde, Oscar, 28
Wilder, Thornton, 14
Wilhelm II, Kaiser, 10

Subject Index

airplanes, 10, 16–17, 31, 35, 45, 50
air raids, 27, 29, 43, 45–46, 50–51
Aisne-Marne canal, 8
Algeria, 8
Allies, 14, 44, 46, 49, 51–52, 54, 62, 65
Alsace, 62
Amerikanismus, 32, 35
Anataios, 77
anti-Semitism, 27, 40–41, 60, 90, 98n29
Arch of Triumph, 19–20, 45
armistice of 1940, 17–18
Arras, 9
Aschaffenburg, 63
assassinations, 3, 23, 25–26, 48–49, 53, 60, 62, 64, 67
Atlantic Wall, 50
atrocities, 36–38, 42, 58–59
Auschwitz, 58
Austria, 12
Autobahn, 32
Avenue des Champs-Élysées, 19, 21, 27, 43
Avenue de Wagram, 20
Avenue Foch, 64, 83
Avenue Kléber, 19, 22, 48, 53, 75, 80
Avenue Malakoff, 83

Baden, 87
Bagatelle Park, 28
Baku, 79
Balkans, 20, 62
Basque territory, 25

Bavaria, 64
Beerhall Putsch of 1923, 40
Belgium, 8, 15–16
Berlin, 11–12, 26, 29, 35, 38, 40–42, 44, 48–49, 53–54, 62–63, 65, 69, 80–81, 84, 87, 102n4
Bible, 23, 33, 36, 47, 51
Black Forest (*Schwarzwald*), 15
Bois de Boulogne, 28–29, 44, 53
Bolschevism, 29
bombing, 28, 44–46, 50–52, 58, 62
Bonn, 80
Bordeaux, 26
Boulevard des Capucines, 20
Boulevard Rochechouart, 23
Boulevard St.-Germain, 51
Boulevard St.-Michel, 28
bourgeoisie, 11,13, 26, 33, 64, 90
Bourges, 18
Brasserie (La) Lorraine, 20–22, 25, 70, 96n2
Bruchsal, 15
Brussels, 8
Buchenwald, 63
Bundeswehr, 21
Burgundy, 9, 51, 64
Byzantium, 51

Café de la Paix, 22, 63
Cambrai, 9
Cannes, 81
Casablanca conference, 65

126 | Subject Index

Caucasus, 36–37, 79
cemeteries, 34, 42: Batignolles, 47, 61; Clichy, 47; Montparnasse, 28, 84; Père Lachaise, 28
Ceylon, 67
champagne, 16, 18, 27, 53, 71
Château-Thierry, 17
Châtenay-Malabry, 22
Chemin des Dames, 17
Cher, Department of, 18
China, 48
Cold War, 37, 68
collaboration (Franco-German), 23, 27, 43, 75, 97n9, 101n15
Cologne, 28, 32, 35
Commandant of Greater Paris, 21
Communist Party (French), 23, 59
Compiègne, 17
concentration camps, 24, 26, 58–59, 63, 84. See also Auschwitz, Buchenwald
Constantinople, 80
Czechoslovakia, 12, 62

Dahlem (Berlin), 35, 38, 48
dandyism, 90–91
Darwinism, 33
deportations, 58, 65. See also Final Solution
Deutsches Literaturarchiv (DLA), 2, 5, 69, 72, 76, 82–83, 88, 95n7. See also Marbach
Domrémy, 18
dreams, 15, 30–32, 36–38, 41, 43, 45, 47, 50, 55, 61–62, 70, 80, 91
Dresden, 58, 62

Egypt, 67
Eiffel Tower, 20
Elbe, 84
England. See Great Britain.
eroticism, 15, 23, 28, 31, 33, 47, 57, 81–82, 95n11. See also sexuality, women
Étoile, 23, 49
Europe, 10, 24, 26, 32, 35, 37, 48–51, 54, 58–59, 65–66, 68, 75
executions, 21–22, 26, 29, 36, 48–49, 58–59, 98n41

fascism, 3, 6, 59–60, 76, 84, 90. See also Nazism
Final Solution, 26, 90
First World War, 2, 5–6, 8–10, 15–18, 36, 40, 51, 54, 56, 62, 73, 83, 90, 103n1

Flanders, 9
flea market (*marché aux puces*), 24
Florence, 52
Foreign Legion, 8–9, 29
France, 8–9, 14–15, 17, 22, 24, 26, 33, 35–37, 40, 43, 45–46, 53–54, 59, 62, 65–67, 71–72, 74, 77–78, 80, 82, 84, 86, 94n13
Frankfurt, 63
French Revolution, 63
Freiburg im Breisgau, 15, 62, 84
Friedrichsthal, 15

Gare de l'Est, 27
Gare d'Orsay, 25
Georgsrunde. See Hotel George V
German Academy of Poetry, 41
German army, 3, 9, 13–22, 26, 28, 34–38, 46, 48, 58–61, 65, 69–70, 74–75, 85, 103n10
German Institute, 69, 71, 74
German language, 1, 4–5, 7
German Literature Archive. See Deutsches Literaturarchiv
Germany, 2–3, 6–8, 10–12, 15, 18, 26, 32, 35, 38–39, 41, 43–46, 48–54, 58, 60, 62–63, 65, 71, 77, 84–85
Gestapo, 24, 49, 64–65, 69, 84
Giessen, 63
Giverny, 53
Goslar, 12
Great Britain, 14, 23, 28, 37, 42, 51, 62–63, 65, 67, 72
Greece, 20, 37, 62
Grunewald (Berlin), 35

Hamburg, 28, 44
Hanover, 7–8, 12, 19, 27, 33, 35–36, 38, 44, 46, 50, 62
Hegelianism, 65
Heidelberg, 7
Hinterzarten, 84
Historikerstreit, 58
Holland. See Netherlands
hostages, 23, 26, 33–34, 36, 42, 59, 65, 69
Hotel Bristol, 77, 83
Hotel Continental, 21, 53
Hôtel de Ville, 20
Hotel George V, 22, 24–25, 42, 64, 69–70, 101n8
Hotel Majestic, 19, 21–23, 27–29, 33, 42, 44–45, 53, 63–64, 69–70, 75, 80, 84

Hotel Raphael, 22, 27, 41–43, 45–49, 51, 53–55, 58, 64, 91
Hotel Ritz, 22, 25, 28, 43, 74
Hungary, 62

Île de la Cité, 28
invasion of 1944. *See* Normandy
Italy, 62, 71

Jardin de Luxembourg, 16
Jardin des Plantes, 21
Jews, 3, 5, 23–24, 26–28, 37, 41–42, 48, 58–59, 63, 65, 84, 98n29, 101n8. *See also* anti-Semitism, deportations, Final Solution
journals. *See* writings by Jünger: *Pariser Tagebücher*

Kaiserreich, 7–8
Kaiserslautern, 16
Kansas City, 97n12
Kapp Putsch, 11
Karlsruhe, 15
Kentucky, 64, 104n15
Kiev, 35, 37, 39, 42
Kirchhorst, 12–13, 15, 18–19, 24–27, 33, 35, 38, 43, 46, 50, 55, 61–63, 70, 80, 85–87, 91
Klett-Cotta Verlag, 2, 67

Lake Constance (*Bodensee*), 12, 67
Laon, 17
La Roche-Guyon, 50–51, 53
Latin Quarter, 28, 47
Left Bank, 21
Leipzig, 11, 49, 73
Le Figaro, 82
Le Monde, 83
Ligne de Sceaux, 27
Limburg, 63
Limoges, 83
Lodz (Litzmannstadt), 48
Loire, 18
London, 43
Longwy, 16
Lorraine, 8–9, 18, 24, 55, 85
Louvre, 16
Lowlands, 15. *See also* Belgium, Netherlands
Luxemburg, 16

Madame, 83
Madeleine, church of, 19, 21, 29, 47

Magdeburg, 84
Maginot Line, 14, 18
Mannheim, 27
Marais (Paris), 63
Marbach am Neckar, 2, 5, 72, 76, 82–83, 88, 95n7
Marne, 17
Marseille, 8, 49
Maubeuge, 8, 19
Maxim's, 27
mechanization, 10, 17, 31–32, 37, 39, 63
Mediterranean, 35
metro (Paris), 43
Metz, 18
military administration. *See* Occupation
Militärbefehlshaber in Frankreich (MBF), 19, 22, 26, 28–29, 33, 49–51, 53, 59, 65, 69, 104n21
Ministry of Propaganda (German), 12
Ministry of War (German), 11
Montmartre, 23, 45, 50, 54
Mont Valérien, 29, 58, 98n41
Morocco, 8
Moselle Valley, 16
Munich, 40, 70
Musée Carnavalet, 63

Nancy, 18
Nantes, 26
Naples, 11
nationalism, 5–6, 11, 41, 50, 71–72
NATO, 21, 70
Nazism, 3, 5–6, 11–12, 24, 28, 40–44, 49, 54, 59–60, 65, 67, 71, 73, 90, 99n13
Nazi Party (NSDAP), 11, 18, 33, 40–41, 58–59, 64, 74, 90
Nazi-Soviet Pact, 23
Netherlands, 10, 15, 62
nihilism, 59
Normandy, 51, 54
North Africa, 20, 35–36, 38–39, 42. *See also* Algeria, Morocco, Tunisia
North Sea, 50
Notre Dame, cathedral of, 20, 27
Nouvelle Revue Française, 24, 76

Occupation, administration of, 2–6, 9, 19, 21–22, 24–26, 29, 34–35, 41–42, 46, 54, 56–57, 59–61, 65–66, 68–72, 74–77, 79, 83–85, 90

Subject Index

Opéra, 20, 22
Operation Torch, 35
Operation Walküre, 53
Orient Express, 80
Ossommes, 17

Paderborn, 63
Palais Royal, 24
Palatinate, 16
Pantheon (Paris), 44
Paris, 2–6, 9, 11, 13, 15–17, 19–30, 35, 37–39, 42–51, 53–57, 59–72, 74–75, 77–88, 90–91
Persia, 37
Peru, 33
Pforzheim, 15
Piper Verlag, 77
Place d'Anvers, 23
Place de la Bastille, 21
Place de la Nation, 20
Place des Invalides, 50
Place des Ternes, 20, 22, 28–29, 70
Place du Tertre, 28
Place Pigalle, 23
Place Vendôme, 22
Pléiade, 94n13
Plon, 76
plot of 20 July 1944, 61–67. *See also* assassinations, Resistance
Poland, 12–14, 26, 62
Pont des Arts, 20
Pont Neuf, 20
Porte de Vincennes, 20
Porte Maillot, 83
prisoners of war (POWs), 16–17, 36
prostitutes, 9, 21
Protestantism, 33
Prussia, 9, 28, 32, 43, 46, 49–50, 62
publishers, 24, 75–76. *See also* Gallimard, Klett-Cotta, Piper, Plon

Quai Louis-Blériot, 25
Quai Voltaire, 26–28

Rambouillet, 28
Ravensburg, 67
Reichswehr, 10–11
Reims, 8, 17
religion, 19, 33, 99n13. *See also* Bible, Protestantism, Roman Catholicism
Renault, 45

Resistance: French, 23, 26, 76; German, 49–51, 71, 101n3, 102n15
restaurants, 27, 37, 42, 47, 70, 91: Restaurant à la Mère Catherine, 28; Boule d'Or (Bourges), 18; Drouant, 22; Tour d'Argent, 27, 42, 71
revolution of 1918, 10, 40
Rhine, 14, 25
Rhodes, 42
Riviera, 83. *See also* Cannes
Robinson, 22
Rochechouart-Barbès metro station, 23
Roman Catholicism, 10, 14, 33
Romanticism, 28, 91
Romilly-sur-Seine, 17
Rostov, 35, 42
Rue de Bellechasse, 25
Rue de Castiglione, 21
Rue de Montpensier, 24
Rue de Rivoli, 21, 45
Rue des Grands-Augustins, 28
Rue du Cherche-Midi, 45, 84, 88
Rue du Faubourg St.-Honoré, 21, 25, 28–29
Rue Lauriston, 80
Rue Mouffetard, 44, 47
Rue Royale, 27
Rue St.-Placide, 45
Russia, 3, 22–23, 25, 29, 32, 34–39, 42, 44, 46–47, 51, 58, 64, 70–71, 83, 85. *See also* Caucasus

Saarbrücken, 18
Sacré Coeur basilica, 20, 29, 54
St.-Denis, 50
St.-Dié, 85
St.-Germain-des-Prés, 26
St.-Quentin, 8, 16–17
St.-Rémy-les-Chevreuses, 27–28
San Francisco, 82
Sarajevo, 25
Sardinia, 67
Sars-Poteries, 19
Scandinavia, 23
Schlachtensee (Berlin), 48
Schlieffen Plan, 15
Schutzstaffel (SS), 48–50, 53, 59
Second World War, 2–3, 5–6, 12, 16, 26, 28–29, 36–37, 41–42, 46, 60, 65–66, 68, 72, 83
Sedan, 16
Seine, 17, 25, 50–51, 57

Service du Travail Obligatoire, 28, 45
Seven Years War, 52
sexuality, 10, 45, 57, 81–82. See also eroticism, women
Sicily, 44
Siegfried Line, 15
Sigmaringen, 67
socialism, 11, 32
Soissons, 17
Somme, battle of, 9, 11
Soviet Union. See Russia
Spain, 25
Speyer, 16
Square du Vert-Galant, 28, 57
Stahlhelm, 40
Stalingrad, battle of, 36, 38, 42
Star of David, 37, 59, 65
Straits of Gibraltar, 25
Strasbourg, 88
Stuttgart, 2, 67
Sumatra, 67
Suresnes, 29, 36, 98n41

Tabarin nightclub, 19
technology. See mechanization
Texas, 37
Third Reich, 33, 37, 42, 60, 64. See also Nazism
Third Republic, 63
Thirty Years War, 60
Tibet, 31
Toul, 18
Toulouse, 80
Tripoli, 38
Trocadéro, 49
Troyes, 18
Tunisia, 36

Überlingen, 12
Ukraine, 38
United States of America, 6, 23, 27, 37, 51, 55, 61–65, 82–83, 102n13

Vaux-les-Cernay, 28, 51
"Vel d'Hiv" razzia, 27–28
Verdun, 8, 54
Versailles treaty, 11, 65
Vichy regime, 17, 23, 35, 75
Vincennes, 20, 22, 28
Völkischer Beobachter, 11
Volkssturm, 61, 85

Wandervogel, 8
Wannsee conference, 26
War of 1870, 15
Weimar Republic, 4–5, 10–12, 41, 63, 90
Weser, 63
West End (Berlin), 35
Wilflingen, 67, 70, 88
Wilhelmshaven, 50
wine, 9, 15–18, 20, 51, 58, 64, 67, 71, 74, 77, 91
women, 3, 9–10, 15, 18, 21–25, 37, 42–44, 57, 67, 71, 79, 81
writings by Jünger: *Auf den Marmorklippen*, 5, 12–13, 26, 28, 33, 53–54, 58, 66, 80, 96n21; *Das abenteuerliche Herz*, 11–12; *Der Arbeiter*, 11, 71; *Der Friede*, 80, 100n19; *Heliopolis*, 5, 66, 104n25; *In Stahlgewittern*, 2, 5, 9–11, 56, 76; *Pariser Tagebücher*, 1–3, 9, 16,18–19, 21–25, 27, 29–30, 32–34, 36–38, 45, 48, 56–60, 63, 65, 67–68, 74, 76, 83, 90–91, 94n7, 99n9; *Strahlungen*, 2, 67, 89

Zirkus Krone, 40